Minehead • Dunster • Blue Anchor • Washford • Watchet • Williton • Stogumber • Heathfield • Crowcombe Heathfield • Bishops Lydeard •

CW01622741

# Stock Book

## And Spotter's Guide

Keith Smith

# Introduction

This is now the 7th edition of the West Somerset Railway Stock Book that I have had the pleasure to compile, and all locomotives, coaching stock, goods wagons and other miscellaneous items resident on the railway, as at January 2016, are fully described. An effort has been made to present a reasonable up-to-date history and technical appraisal of all items in the collection wherever possible.

With such a large operational railway, changes in the rolling stock register are frequent – new items arrive, while others depart, some are stored for overhaul, while others are restored to their former glory. Overall, the gains outweigh the losses, so for each edition of this publication my task has become just that little more involved. The efforts of the railway's staff – paid and volunteer alike – who restore and maintain the various items of rolling stock are very much in evidence, the standard achieved being a credit to their craftsmanship and enthusiasm.

This Stock Book is intended to complement the official *West Somerset Railway Guide Book*, which I recommend for your further reading. I sincerely hope that you enjoy your visit to the West Somerset Railway, and that this publication gives you a deeper understanding of both the train in which you travel and of the other items you see on your trip. If you have any comments about this publication, can provide additional information, or correct any inaccuracies, I would be pleased to hear from you, care of The Railway Station, Minehead, Somerset, TA24 5BG.

*Left:* Minehead servicing facility as seen on 13 March 2008 – not the best day weather-wise! *Peter Townsend*

# Map of the West Somerset Railway

# Acknowledgements

This publication would not be possible without the assistance of many people, either in supplying data, photographs, or general help and assistance. I am proud to publicly acknowledge their contribution. Grateful thanks are also extended to the photographers whose work is included, and who are individually credited alongside each illustration.

Above all, however, I must thank you, the reader, for purchasing this book, and making all the effort worthwhile.

Keith Smith
January 2016

# Locomotives

There is an interesting and varied fleet of locomotives – both steam and heritage diesel – based on the West Somerset Railway. The vast majority have a Great Western Railway or British Railways Western Region 'flavour', in keeping with the WSR Company's aim 'to recreate, for present and future generations, a typical West Country branch line by providing a working museum atmosphere based principally upon the traditions of the GWR.'

The majority of the railway's services are steam-hauled. There is currently a fleet of ex-BR 'main-line' locomotives based on the line, though not all are in service at any one time. These include one of the two surviving Somerset & Dorset 2-8-0 freight engines, No 53808, and the unique 2-6-0 tender engine, No 9351, which was completely rebuilt from a GWR 'Large Prairie' tank in the railway's own workshops at Minehead.

Heritage diesel traction is used to support the steam fleet on passenger services, notably at off-peak periods. Normal timetabled services are usually worked by a diesel multiple unit (DMU). Diesel locomotives are used on a wide variety of work on the WSR, including engineering trains, charter work and at special events. The diesel fleet on the line includes one of the popular 'Western' and two 'Hymek' diesel-hydraulics.

The 'in-house' fleet is supported by a number of 'guest' engines during the course of the year, some of which are hired in for a particular special event, while others – such as GWR 2-6-2T No 5553 – have spent much longer periods based on the line. This also creates added interest. Visitors have included the last ever steam engine constructed by British Railways, 9F 2-10-0 No 92220 *Evening Star*, the world-famous GWR 4-4-0 No 3440 *City of Truro*, the unique BR 8P 'Pacific' No 71000 *Duke of Gloucester* and GWR 'King' Class 4-6-0 No 6024 *King Edward I*.

In this first section of the Stock Book the locomotives are largely arranged in numerical order, so far as the 'main-line' types are concerned, with the diesels following after the steam.

A visitor to the WSR at the 2012 Spring Gala was BR Standard Class 4-6-2 No 70000 *Britannia*, seen here on the Minehead turntable. *Peter Rowlands*

# Former main-line steam locomotives

## 4110 GWR 2-6-2T

Locomotive No 4110 at Minehead. *Keith Smith*

### Time Line

**Built:** October 1936
Swindon Works

**Known shed allocations:**
1936 Severn Tunnel Junction
1942 Birkenhead
1943 Birmingham area
1962 Taunton
1963-5 Neath and Radyr
1965 Severn Tunnel Junction

**Withdrawn:** August 1965

**Rescued:** May 1979

**Arrival at WSR:** 2015

No 4110 is a sister locomotive to No 4160, which has been on the West Somerset Railway since 1990. As one of a class of locomotives that were to total 140, No 4110 from one of a batch of ten built at Swindon Works in October 1936 to Lot 292 and Diagram A9. It was dispatched to its first shed allocation – Severn Tunnel Junction – in October for use on tunnel banking duties, but this was short-lived as two months later it was moved to the Wolverhampton District, where it stayed for the next 26 years. No 4110's work consisted of operating the intensive local passenger services from Birmingham's Snow Hill and Moor Street stations to Leamington, Stratford-upon-Avon and Warwickshire in general. March 1942 to April 1943 saw a move to Birkenhead, but then the engine migrated back to the Birmingham District. Eventually in June 1962 No 4110 arrived at Taunton shed, being employed for the first time as a Minehead branch engine. A year later it was in South Wales, working out of Neath, then Radyr, and finally in April 1965 back to the shed where it started its working life, Severn Tunnel Junction. Withdrawn two months later, the engine arrived at Woodham Brothers' famous Barry scrapyard in August 1965, having run in excess of 730,000 miles in revenue-earning service.

A new era in No 4110's life came

in 1979, when it was purchased for preservation by the Great Western Preservation Group at Southall, leaving Barry in May of that year and becoming the 100th locomotive to do so. Moved to the Birmingham Railway Museum at Tyseley for contract restoration, only a partial amount of work was carried out before the owners decided to put the engine up for sale, releasing funds to enable restoration and completion of their pannier tank No 9682. Against competition, WSR Plc was the successful purchaser, and No 4110 duly arrived at Minehead on 16 June 2015. Minor cosmetic work has been done, but full restoration work will not commence until the overhauls of both Nos 9351 and 53808 are complete.

Technical details for this locomotive are as for No 4160 below.

Locomotive No 4110 at Minehead buffer stops carrying a banner seeking support for the restoration that lies ahead. *Keith Smith*

# 4160 BR(W) 2-6-2T

No 4160 is seen at Watchet carrying the British Railways 'lion & wheel' logo on the side tanks. *Keith Smith*

## Time Line

**Built:** October 1948
Swindon Works

**Known shed allocations:**
1948 Barry
1954 Rhymney
1956 Radyr
1962 Stored out of use
1963 Radyr
196? Severn Tunnel Junction

**Withdrawn:** June 1965

**Rescued:** May 1974

**Arrival at WSR:** 1990

Originally designed by the Chief Mechanical Engineer of the Great Western Railway, G. J. Churchward, and perpetuated by his successor C. B. Collett, more than 300 of the 'Large Prairie' tank locomotives were built from 1909 until 1948. No 4160 was the first member of the last batch of 20 locomotives of the '5101' Class, Nos 4160-79, built between 1948 and 1949 by British Railways immediately following nationalisation. It was the first engine of Lot 3369, and cost £8,190, which included £1,553 for the boiler (No 8810); it was turned out in unlined green livery lettered 'BRITISH RAILWAYS' on the tank sides.

All of its working life appears to have been spent in South Wales, initially allocated to Barry, where it was sent new on 28 October 1948 and was frequently seen on the local passenger services to Merthyr and Treherbert. No 4160 received a Heavy Intermediate overhaul at Stafford Road, Wolverhampton, from 5 July 1951, lasting 57 days, before returning to Barry shed. This was followed by a Light Intermediate repair at Caerphilly Works. In January 1954 No 4160 was transferred to Rhymney shed, a sub-shed of Merthyr, principally working local services along the valley to Caerphilly and Cardiff. Further overhauls followed at Swindon in 1954 (Heavy General, with boiler No 8824 fitted) and Caerphilly in 1956 (Heavy Intermediate).

The 'Large Prairie' was transferred to Radyr shed on 20 May 1956, where it continued the same kind of work as before. It received a further Heavy General overhaul at Caerphilly in 1958/59, when boiler No 8811 was fitted. No 4160 was put into store in September 1962, due to a shortage of work – principally caused by the

Resting between turns, No 4160 is seen at Minehead during the 2008 Spring Gala. *Peter Townsend*

introduction of diesel multiple units – before returning to Radyr on 25 March 1963. Surprisingly, the 2-6-2T received a further Heavy General repair, its last, at Swindon in September 1962, when boiler No 8819 was fitted. No 4160 finished its BR career at Severn Tunnel Junction, working on the gruelling tunnel banking duties before its inevitable withdrawal from service on 3 June 1965, whereupon it was sold to Woodham Brothers' at Barry, arriving there in August 1965.

No 4160 was initially purchased for preservation by the Birmingham Railway Museum at Tyseley, departing from Barry in August 1974. However, little restoration work was carried out, and a subsequent change in policy resulted in the engine being put up for sale by the BRM in 1981. It was subsequently bought for use on the embryonic Plym Valley Railway by a consortium of shareholders, moving initially to the Plymouth Exhibition Centre at Millbay in May 1981, then to the PVR's Marsh Mills site in March 1982. Restoration was commenced, and the locomotive stripped down.

In 1989 the owner, 4160 Limited, decided that the interest of the locomotive would be better served by moving it to a new home on an established railway for restoration to be completed. A share scheme was set up enabling the WSR Association to become a major shareholder in the engine. No 4160 arrived at Minehead as a kit of parts on 12 April 1990.

Full restoration work commenced in the autumn of 1990, the driving wheels and axleboxes being sent to Swindon for attention. By June 1991 the chassis had been rewheeled, and by September 1992 a mobile set of frames complete with motion and brake gear was evident. A 'running-in' trip was made to Blue Anchor on 4 October 1992, and throughout the winter work was concentrated on the boiler. A successful steam test was

No 4160 is seen here at Bishops Lydeard in the early, and for this locomotive the original, British Railways livery on the side tanks. *WSR Collection*

undertaken on 2 February 1993, and the boiler was reunited with the frames ten days later. On 22-23 1993 a fire was lit in No 4160's firebox and the engine ran under its own power for the first time since 1965.

The locomotive formally entered service on the WSR on 6 August 1993, in time to star at the WSRA's annual Steam Fayre & Vintage Vehicle Rally event, double-heading with No 4561. Restored initially in BR lined black livery, complete with the BR 'cycling lion' emblem on the tank sides, after five years it was repainted in unlined green, with 'BRITISH RAILWAYS' on its tank sides, the livery it carried when first built. The 2-6-2T has proved a very reliable and popular performer, capable of handling eight-coach trains with ease.

After ten years of very successful service on the WSR – where it had accumulated a total mileage of 85,841 – No 4160 was withdrawn from service on 7 June 2003, upon expiry of its ten-year boiler certificate and after working a special train for shareholders. The locomotive was immediately dispatched to the Buckfastleigh workshops of the South Devon Railway where arrangements had been finalised for a contract overhaul. On arrival, a complete stripdown took place, with the boiler being sent to LNWR at Crewe for repair.

On 8 August 2006 the locomotive entered service on the SDR for running-in, followed by a loan to the Mid-Hants Railway before returning to the WSR. At the end of the 2015 Winter Steam Festival, the locomotive was again withdrawn from service on the expiry of the ten-year boiler certificate, and was immediately taken to the workshops of the Llangollen Railway for overhaul.

| | |
|---|---|
| Tractive effort | 23,400lb |
| Boiler pressure | 200lbs/sq in |
| Power class | D |
| Route availability | Blue |
| Weight (in full working order): | 78t 9cwt |
| Weight (empty) | 66t 0cwt |
| Length | 41ft 0ins |
| Total wheelbase | 31ft 9ins |
| Coupled wheelbase | 14ft 9ins |
| Width | 8ft 11½ins |
| Height | 12ft 11½ins |
| Wheel diameter (pony truck) | 3ft 2ins |
| Wheel diameter (driving) | 5ft 8ins |
| Boiler diameter | 4ft 5½ins - 5ft 0½ins |

| | |
|---|---|
| Number of tubes | 218 |
| Length of tubes | 11ft 0ins |
| Tube heating surface | 1,145 sq ft |
| Grate area | 20.3 sq ft |
| Firebox surface area | 121 sq ft |
| Number of flues | 6 |
| Superheater surface area | 82 sq ft |
| Cylinders | 18ins x 30ins (2 Outside) |
| Valve gear | Stephenson (Inside) |
| Coal capacity | 4t |
| Water capacity | 2,000 gallons |
| Maximum axle load | 17t 12cwt |

# 4561

## GWR 2-6-2T

### Time Line

**Built:** October 1924
Swindon Works

**Known shed allocations:**
1924 Tyseley
1927 Newport Ebbw Junction
1930-38 Plymouth (both Laira and Millbay), Launceston, Moorswater, Bodmin, St. Blazey, Exeter, and Penzance
1938 Truro
1958 Newton Abbot
1961 Plymouth Laira

**Withdrawn:** May 1962

**Rescued:** May 1975

**Arrival at WSR:** 1975

The Great Western Railway's '45xx' Class was derived from the '44xx' Class of 2-6-2Ts already in service on some of the West Country branch lines in the first decade of the 20th century. The latter were, however, too slow for some of the faster services then being timetabled, and it was decided to build a new batch of 'Small Prairie' tank locomotives with slightly larger driving wheels. The first 20 were built at Wolverhampton during 1906-08 (Lot No N3), with running numbers 2161-80. Construction was then transferred to Swindon Works, with the next batch being Nos 2181-90 from 1909. The first 30 were later renumbered as Nos 4500-29. A further 45 members of the class were built, and could be distinguished from the earlier members by the curved running plate at the front end. Several other modifications were also made.

No 4561 was built in Swindon Works in October 1924 under Lot No 226 at a cost of £3,802. It was sent new to Tyseley shed on the southern outskirts of Birmingham, where it principally worked outer-suburban services to Leamington Spa and Stratford-upon-Avon. During September 1927 it moved to Newport (Ebbw Junction), again for use on local passenger trains in that part of Wales.

In 1930 the 'Small Prairie' began what was to become an unbroken spell of 32 years working on various lines in Devon and Cornwall. Between 1930 and 1938 it became a very unsettled locomotive, spending time at Plymouth (both Laira and Millbay), Launceston, Moorswater, Bodmin, St Blazey, Exeter and Penzance. During this time it would have worked GWR branch-line services to Tavistock, Launceston, Looe, Wadebridge, Newquay, Heathfield, Tiverton, Dulverton and St Ives. However, in September 1938 No 4561 found a more permanent home working out of Truro shed. From there it became a regular on services on the Falmouth branch, on the Truro to Newquay line (via Chacewater), and other stopping trains over the Cornish main line.

Twenty years later, in November 1958, the 2-6-2T moved to Newton Abbot shed, where it established itself as a 'regular', working passenger and goods trains on the Brent to

No 4561 after withdrawal in 1998 and awaiting resoration is seen here at Minehead. *WSR Collection*

Kingsbridge branch. The locomotive was displaced from that line in the spring of 1961 following the introduction of diesel multiple units, when it spent a few weeks working the local goods trains on the Dart Valley line between Totnes and Ashburton. No 4561 ended up at Plymouth Laira shed – working primarily on trains to Tavistock and Launceston – before withdrawal in May 1962, having achieved a total recorded mileage of 997,635. The locomotive was sold to Woodhams' scrapyard at Barry, arriving there in July 1962.

After 13 years languishing at Barry awaiting the arrival of the cutter's torch, No 4561 was rescued by the West Somerset Railway Association, together with Nos 5521 and 5542. Transport haulier Mike Laurence moved the three 'Small Prairie' tanks to Bishops Lydeard in September 1975. No 4561 eventually moved on to Minehead for restoration to commence. However, due to the pressure of other work, including the need to complete an overhaul on No 6412, which lasted for five years, the restoration of the 2-6-2T was laid aside, but recommenced at the end of 1984.

Restoration gathered momentum during the mid-1980s. The frames were dispatched to the Severn Valley Railway for repair during 1986 and, on their return, the boiler made a similar journey. Meanwhile, at Minehead the WSRA Locomotive Department was rebuilding the bottom half to create a rolling chassis, while a separate team from the Association's Bristol Area Group was fabricating a new bunker and side tanks at Bitton. The boiler was refitted to the frames in March 1989.

On 15 August 1989 No 4561 was steamed for the first time since its withdrawal in 1962 and, after a number of running-in trips, was introduced to traffic at the WSR's Gala Week hauling a demonstration freight train. Following final painting in its original unlined Brunswick Green, the locomotive formally entered traffic and passenger service on 14 October 1989, restoration having cost £100,000. By New Year's Day 1990 the 'Small Prairie' had clocked up its first trouble-free 1,000 miles.

No 4561 subsequently proved itself to be a reliable and popular performer on the WSR. In addition it has visited a number of other preserved lines the Bluebell Railway (February-March 1996); the North Norfolk Railway (April 1996); the Bodmin & Wenford Railway (August-September 1996); and the South

No 4561 at Bishops Lydeard. *The late Peter Thompson/Keith Smith Collections*

Devon Railway (September-October 1996).

In 1998 the 'Small Prairie' was painted in BR unlined black livery to spend the season working trains on the South Devon Railway again, returning to the WSR in the autumn. After working 47,834 miles on the WSR, No 4561 was withdrawn from service in November of that year for its statutory ten-year overhaul, which was not planned to commence until the restoration of No 34046 *Braunton* was completed. This work is now under way at Williton, and involves a complete new set of frames due to the originals being beyond further use.

No 4561 on static display in the town of its birth at STEAM Museum, Swindon, 16 November 2007. *M. J. Stretton*

| | |
|---|---|
| Tractive effort | 21,250lb |
| Boiler pressure | 200lbs/sq in |
| Power class | C |
| Route availability | Yellow |
| Weight (in full working order): | 57t 0cwt |
| Weight (empty) | 49t 15cwt |
| Length | 36ft 4½ins |
| Total wheelbase | 26ft 10ins |
| Coupled wheelbase | 11ft 6ins |
| Width | 8ft 9½ins |
| Height | 13ft 0½ins |
| Wheel diameter (pony truck) | 3ft 2ins |
| Wheel diameter (driving) | 4ft 7½ins |
| Boiler diameter | 4ft 2ins - 4ft 9½ins |

| | |
|---|---|
| Number of tubes | 218 |
| Length of tubes | 11ft 0ins |
| Tube heating surface | 992 sq ft |
| Grate area | 16.6 sq ft |
| Firebox surface area | 95 sq ft |
| Number of flues | 6 |
| Superheater surface area | 78 sq ft |
| Cylinders | 17ins x 24ins (2 Outside) |
| Valve gear | Stephenson (Inside) |
| Coal capacity | 3½t |
| Water capacity | 950 gallons |
| Maximum axle load | 14t 10cwt |

# 4936 GWR 4-6-0 *Kinlet Hall*

In 1924 'Saint' Class locomotive No 2925 *Saint Martin* was taken into Swindon Works to be modified with larger driving wheels, a lowered boiler and a 'Castle' Class-style cab. The 'Hall' Class was born.

No 4936 was built in Swindon in June 1929 to a C. B. Collett design, and become one of a class that was to eventually number 330, including the subsequent 'Modified Halls', such as No 6960 (see below). Build costs amounted to £5,209, which included £1,167 for the boiler and £834 for the tender. Its first shed was Chester, followed by allocations to Shrewsbury, Oxley, and Wolverhampton (Stafford Road), before transfer to Oxford in 1933. Moving next to Banbury and Old Oak Common, April saw a move to the West Country, initially at Truro. However, in 1941, while at Plymouth, a

## Time Line

**Built:** June 1929
Swindon Works

**Known shed allocations:**
1929-33 Chester, Shrewsbury Oxley, Wolverhampton (SR)
1933 Oxford, Banbury, Old Oak Common
1933 Truro,
1941 Newton Abbot Works
1954 Plymouth Laira
1958 Newton Abbot
1962 Cardiff

**Withdrawn:** January 1964

**Rescued:** May 1981

**Arrival at WSR:** May 2014

Looking resplendent in the early spring sunshine, GWR 4-6-0 No 4936 *Kinlet Hall* is captured at Eastcombe on 26 March 2015 during the WSR Spring Steam Gala. *Sylvia Way*

heavy bombing raid took place and *Kinlet Hall* was severely damaged by falling into a bomb crater. This caused extensive damage to the bogie and main frames but, because of the locomotive shortage at the time, repairs were authorised, and these were carried out at Newton Abbot Works. Still based in the West Country, No 4936 was transferred to Plymouth Laira in October 1954, then to Newton Abbot in 1958.

With dieselisation taking place, *Kinlet Hall* was moved to Cardiff in May 1962, operating out of both Canton and East Docks sheds. Withdrawn in January 1964, it arrived at Woodhams' Barry scrapyard in June of that year, having run a total of 1,339,061 miles in service. Rescue come as a result of a purchase by a private group in 1979, and in May 1981 No 4936 became the 126th locomotive to leave Barry, and was transported to Peak Rail at Matlock. In 1985 it left for the Gloucestershire Warwickshire Railway, but was subsequently moved to the Birmingham Railway Museum at Tyseley. A milestone was reached on 16 February 2000 when No 4936 had a successful steam test, and main-line certification followed on 8 June.

A general overhaul took place in November 2009, after another 22,154 miles in service, returning to traffic in 2011. Arriving on the WSR in May 2014, an agreement has since been made with the locomotive's owner, The Kinlet Hall 4936 Society, whereby it will remain on the West Somerset for a further five years, making Minehead the locomotive's home shed, although it will be available to work main-line charters if required.

The building Kinlet Hall is a Grade I listed 18th-century English country house at Kinlet, Shropshire, originally the family home of the Childe family, but now an independent day and residential school.

| | |
|---|---|
| Tractive effort | 27,275lb |
| Boiler pressure | 225lbs/sq in |
| Power class | D (5MT) |
| Route availability | Red |
| Weight (in full working order): | 75t 0cwt |
| Weight (empty) | 69t 0cwt |
| Length | 63ft 0ins |
| Total wheelbase | 27ft 3ins |
| Coupled wheelbase | 14ft 9ins |
| Width | 8ft 11½ins |
| Height | 13ft 0¼ins |
| Wheel diameter (driving) | 6ft 0ins |
| Wheel diameter (pony truck) | 3ft 0ins |
| Boiler | GWR No 1 Taper |

| | |
|---|---|
| Number of tubes | 176 |
| Length of tubes | 14ft 10ins |
| Tube heating surface | 1686.6 sq ft |
| Grate area | 27 sq ft |
| Firebox surface area | 155 sq ft |
| Number of flues | 6 |
| Superheater surface area | 262.62 sq ft |
| Cylinders | 18½ins x 30ins (2 Outside) |
| Valve gear | Stephenson (Inside) |
| Coal capacity | 6t |
| Water capacity | 4,000 gallons |
| Maximum axle load | 18t 9cwt |

# 6960 GWR 4-6-0 *Raveningham Hall*

No 6960 looking resplendent in the sunshine at Minehead buffer stops awaits its next turn. *Peter Townsend*

## Time Line

**Built:** March 1944
Swindon Works

**Known shed allocations:**
1944 Old Oak Common
1953 Reading
1963 Oxford

**Withdrawn:** June 1964

**Rescued:** May 1972

**Arrival at WSR:** 2011

Introduced in 1944 to a modification by F.W. Hawksworth of Collett's successful mixed-traffic design, *Raveningham Hall* is a member of the 'Modified Hall' or '6959' Class. A number of improvements were made to the original design, including superheating the boiler, which enabled the locomotives to be more free-running and better steamers, making them compatible with the 'Castle' Class. The only real visual difference between a 'Hall' and a 'Modified Hall' is that the latter is fitted with a plate frame bogie, hence the plate between the frames when viewed from the front.

Our example is the second of a batch of 12 to be completed at Swindon before production was halted due to the war, not resuming until 1947. Because of wartime restrictions on metal, it was not until June 1947 that the name *Raveningham Hall* was bestowed on the locomotive. Its first shed allocation was Old Oak Common, transferring to Reading in 1953, then Oxford ten years later in August 1963. Withdrawn from service in June 1964, it arrived at Barry scrapyard a month later, residing there until 1972, when it was purchased for preservation by the directors of Steamtown, Carnforth, where it moved in October of that year. A complete overhaul followed, and *Raveningham Hall* was one of the few GWR representatives to take part in the Rail 150 cavalcade at Shildon in 1975. Moved to the Severn Valley Railway in that year, it was privately purchased in 1977, and transferred to the Gloucestershire Warwickshire Railway in 1996, where it remained until expiry of the boiler certificate in 2003; No 6960's last rostered duty was to convey HRH The Princess Royal from Winchcombe to Cheltenham Racecourse on 7 April. The locomotive was then dispatched to Bill Parker's Flour Mill workshops in the Forest of Dean for an extensive overhaul, this being completed at Williton in November 2011. *Ravenigham Hall* is now a resident of the West Somerset Railway on long-term hire.

The building Raveningham Hall is the principal house on the Raveningham Estate situated just south of Norwich, and is Grade II listed. Built around 1750 for Sir Edmund Bacon, it is not normally open to the public, although the estate gardens are, and it is now home to Sir Nicholas Bacon.

| | |
|---|---|
| Tractive effort | 27,275lb |
| Boiler pressure | 225lbs/sq in |
| Power class | D |
| Route availability | Red |
| Locomotive weight (in full working order) | 75t 16cwt |
| Weight locomotive (empty) | 70t 4cwt |
| Tender weight (in full working order) | 47t 6cwt |
| Total length | 63ft 0ins |
| Total wheelbase | 27ft 3ins |
| Coupled wheelbase | 14ft 9ins |
| Width | 8ft 11½ins |
| Height | 13ft 2ins |
| Wheel diameter (pony truck) | 3ft 0ins |
| Wheel diameter (driving) | 6ft 0ins |

| | |
|---|---|
| Boiler | GWR No 1 Taper |
| Number of tubes | 176 |
| Length of tubes | 14ft 10ins |
| Tube heating surface | 1582.6 sq ft |
| Grate area | 27.07 sq ft |
| Firebox surface area | 154.9 sq ft |
| Number of flues | 6 |
| Superheater surface area | 295 sq ft |
| Cylinders | 18½ins x 30ins (2 Outside) |
| Valve gear | Stephenson (Inside) |
| Coal capacity | 6t |
| Water capacity | 4,000 gallons |
| Maximum axle load | 18t 9cwt |

No 6960 coasts into Blue Anchor under cloudy skies with a service to Bishops Lydeard. *Keith Smith*

# 7821 BR(W) 4-6-0 *Ditcheat Manor*

Designed by C. B. Collett, the 'Manor' Class 4-6-0s were introduced by the Great Western Railway in 1938. They were a lightweight version of the 'Hall' and 'Grange' classes, and the first 20 incorporated parts from a batch of withdrawn Churchward 2-6-0s. The 'Manors' were built in Swindon Works in two batches – Nos 7800-19 in 1938/39 by the GWR, followed by Nos 7820-29 in 1950 by British Railways after nationalisation. The new standard No 14 boiler was used in their construction, but initially it was found not to be a good steamer, until trials with No 7818 during 1951/52 showed serious draughting problems. Once this was rectified, the 'Manors' performed very successfully, seeing widespread use on both the Cambrian section in Wales, and in the West Country.

## Time Line

**Built:** November 1950 Swindon Works

**Known shed allocations:**
- 1950 Oswestry
- 1953 Shrewsbury
- 1953 Tyseley
- 1959 Newton Abbot
- 1961 Croes Newydd
- 1963-65 Machynlleth, Oxley, Shrewsbury

**Withdrawn:** November 1965

**Rescued:** June 1981

**Arrival at WSR:** 2007

*Ditcheat Manor* emerged from Swindon Works in November 1950, under Lot No 377 to Diagram A9, at a cost of £10,479. The first shed allocation was Oswestry, where the loco found employment on the mid-Wales services to Aberystwyth. Three years later a reallocation to Shrewsbury took place, but by December 1953 Tyseley was its new home, where it was recorded working Oxley to Pontypool Road freight traffic. However,

*Opposite page:* No 7821 *Ditcheat Manor* is seen at Norton Fitzwarren with ex-GWR carriages; there is much activity in the adjacent car park! *Keith Smith*
*Above:* No 7821 is seen at STEAM Museum, Swindon, where the 'Manor' will be on static display until restration to running condition can be undertaken. *Keith Smith*

for a week in January 1955 No 7821 was observed on local Thames Valley services from Paddington. In the summer of 1959 it joined several classmates at Newton Abbot shed for a two-year stint working services over the South Devon banks. During September 1961 *Ditcheat Manor* was back in Wales at Croes Newydd shed, then on to Machynlleth in March 1963 for Cambrian line duties. Short allocations followed at Oxley and Shrewsbury again before being withdrawn from service in November 1965. Arriving at Barry scrapyard in May 1966, it remained there for 15 years before being purchased in 1980 by Ken Ryder; leaving in June 1981, it became the 132nd locomotive to do so.

Initially moved to the Gloucester Warwickshire Railway, and later to the Llangollen Railway, *Ditcheat Manor* was moved to Swindon for restoration, which was completed in 1998. This enabled it to come to the West Somerset Railway for running-in turns and an appearance at that year's Autumn Steam Gala. Moving to the Great Central Railway and the Churnet Valley Railway, it was put up for sale in 2007. Now owned by the West Somerset Railway Association, the locomotive went to Crewe Heritage Centre for an assessment with a view to extending the recently expired ten-year boiler certificate for up to another two years. However, this was not granted, so the locomotive was returned to the WSR. As No 4561 was in Williton Works for its own ten-year overhaul, No 7821 has been granted a place within the STEAM Museum at Swindon for public display and warm storage until such time as it can be accommodated in Williton.

The building Ditcheat Manor is a 17th-century house built by Sir Ralph Horton, and is Grade II listed. Situated in the centre of the village of Ditcheat, Somerset, it is privately owned with no public access.

Technical details are as for No 7828 below.

# 7828 BR(W) 4-6-0 *Odney Manor*

The driver of No 7828 *Odney Manor* checks his pocket watch, and chats to a member of staff, while awaiting departure from Crowcombe Heatfield. *WSR Collection*

## Time Line

**Built:** October 1950
Swindon Works

**Known shed allocations:**
1951 In store
1951 Neath
1952 Shrewsbury
1961 Croes Newydd
1963 Aberystwyth
1963 Shrewsbury

**Withdrawn:** October 1965

**Rescued:** June 1981

**Arrival at WSR:** 1995

This is the second of the 'Manor' Class engines to be based on the West Somerset Railway and – like No 7820 *Dinmore Manor* – was a member of the second batch of locomotives (Nos 7820-29), built by British Railways (Western Region) in 1950. *Odney Manor* was the penultimate member of the class, completed at Swindon in December 1950, to Lot 377, at a cost of £10,425. After the usual period of running-in, the engine was, surprisingly, placed in store at the start of 1951. However, in February of that year it re-entered service based at Neath shed for use on secondary duties in the Swansea area. During December 1952 No 7828 commenced an extended period of operation on the lines of the former Cambrian Railways, initially allocated to Shrewsbury shed, where it remained for nine years. During this time it became a frequent choice to work the 'Cambrian Coast Express' between Shrewsbury and Aberystwyth, but also worked local passenger and goods trains in the Shrewsbury area. While at Shrewsbury the 'Manor' received three major repairs – a Heavy Intermediate at Wolverhampton (November-December 1953), a Heavy General at Swindon (June-July 1956) and a Heavy Intermediate, also at Swindon (June to September 1959).

*Odney Manor* was transferred to Croes Newydd shed in May 1961 for use on services in the Wrexham area, where it was principally deployed on workings from Chester and Wrexham to Barmouth and Pwllheli (via Ruabon and Llangollen). However, it did stray from its

Resting at Minehead, No 7828 *Odney Manor* has the look of a locomotive that has arrived on a service train during the 1950s, such is the realism that brings back so many memories for people of a certain age. *Keith Smith*

own patch on occasions, even being noted on a goods train at Stratford-upon-Avon. A further Heavy General repair took place at Swindon (June-September 1962), followed by a new allocation to Aberystwyth shed in March 1963. While there *Odney Manor* would have worked services to Carmarthen, Shrewsbury and Oswestry. A move back to Shrewsbury occurred in August 1963, which proved to be its last, as No 7828 was condemned on 2 October 1965, its recorded mileage being 402,613. The 'Manor' was subsequently brought by Woodhams' scrapyard, and moved there in May 1966.

Privately purchased in June 1981, the locomotive was moved initially to the infant Gloucester Warwickshire Railway, together with No 7821 *Ditcheat Manor*. The engine was steamed again on 11 December 1987, before spending a brief period on hire to the Gwili Railway in South Wales, followed by a more permanent move to Llangollen. *Odney Manor* then moved on to unfamiliar territory on the East Lancashire Railway. No 7828 moved by road to the WSR on 25 April 1995, initially for a year. It was sent to Swindon for repairs, returning in May 1998 and becoming a regular performer on WSR trains. However, in August 2002 a tube problem was found and, as the locomotive was near the end of its ten-year boiler certificate, it was decided to withdraw it from service pending a decision on its future. The owner subsequently put No 7828 up for sale, and it was purchased by the WSR plc to secure its future, the agreement being completed on 13 May 2004. No 7828 entered the workshop at Minehead in November of that year, the boiler being removed for dispatch to LNWR at Crewe on the same vehicle that brought in No 53808's overhauled boiler. On completion of the overhaul, No 7828 was temporary renamed in 2011 as *Norton Manor (40 Commando)* as a tribute to the Marines based at Norton Manor camp, just south of Bishops Lydeard.

As a footnote, unlike the rest of the class names there is no building actually called 'Odney Manor'. It would appear that the Swindon researchers got it wrong, as the manor house they assumed to bear the name was in fact Lilleshall Manor, which stands in Odney Lane, Lilleshall, near Cookham.

| | |
|---|---|
| Tractive effort | 27,340lb |
| Boiler pressure | 200lbs/sq in |
| Power class | D |
| Route availability | Blue |
| Locomotive weight (in full working order) | 68t 18cwt |
| Weight locomotive (empty) | 63t 6cwt |
| Tender weight (in full working order) | 40t 0cwt |
| Tender weight (empty) | 18t 15cwt |
| Length (locomotive) | 37ft 4½ins |
| Length(tender) | 24ft 4½ins |
| Total length | 61ft 9ins |
| Total wheelbase | 52ft 1½ins |
| Coupled wheelbase | 14ft 9ins |
| Width | 8ft 11ins |
| Height | 12ft 8½ins |
| Wheel diameter (pony truck) | 3ft 0ins |

| | |
|---|---|
| Wheel diameter (driving) | 5ft 8ins |
| Wheel diameter (tender) | 4ft 1½ins |
| Boiler diameter | 4ft 7½ins |
| Number of tubes | 158 |
| Length of tubes | 12ft 0ins |
| Tube heating surface | 1,285 sq ft |
| Grate area | 22.1 sq ft |
| Firebox surface area | 140 sq ft |
| Number of flues | 12 |
| Superheater surface area | 190 sq ft |
| Cylinders | 18ins x 30ins (2 Outside) |
| Valve gear | Stephenson (Inside) |
| Coal capacity | 6t |
| Water capacity | 3,500 gallons |
| Maximum axle load | 17t 5cwt |

# 9351 WSR 2-6-0 (ex-GWR 2-6-2T No 5193)

Seen here at Minehead is the WSR rebuild No 9351 which started life as a '5101' Class tank engine but has been transformed to a 'Mogul'. *Keith Smith*

## Time Line
**No 5193**

**Built:** October 1934
Swindon Works

**Known shed allocations:**
1934 Stourbridge Junction
1939 Wolverhampton Oxley
1939 Stourbridge Junction
1952-60 Truro, St. Blazey, and Plymouth Laira
1960 Neyland

**Withdrawn:** June 1962

**Rescued:** May 1979

**Arrival at WSR:** 1998

**Rebuilt as 9351 'Mogul' by WSR:** 2001-2004

Also, like No 4160, a member of the '5101' Class, No 5193 was built by the Great Western Railway at Swindon in October 1934 – 14 years before No 4160 – and was sent new to Stourbridge Junction shed in the West Midlands. Stourbridge had a large fleet of these 2-6-2Ts, primarily for use on suburban passenger services to Birmingham Snow Hill and Wolverhampton Low Level, an area with which the class was long associated. Apart from a short stay at Oxley shed, Wolverhampton, between July and September 1939, No 5193 remained at Stourbridge for 18 years.

The 'Large Prairie' moved to the West Country in October 1952, staying for varying lengths of time at Truro, St Blazey and Plymouth Laira sheds. The engine worked on passenger and freight trains on several lines in the area, and performed regularly on the Par-Newquay branch during its time at St Blazey. During May 1956 – when the turntable at Penzance shed was undergoing repair – No 5193, together with other members of the class, was employed on express passenger trains to and from Penzance, thus avoiding tender-first running by main-line engines.

With many services in the South West being transferred to diesel multiple units during the late 1950s and early 1960s, No 5193 moved on to Neyland shed in November 1960. It appeared on a mixture of duties in the Tenby and Pembroke areas before condemnation in June 1962, and subsequent storage at Severn Tunnel Junction (from where No 4160 was also withdrawn). The locomotive was sold to Woodhams' scrapyard at Barry, arriving there in October 1962.

After languishing in the scrapyard for 17 years – longer than its ownership with both the GWR and British Railways – No 5193 was purchased by the '5193 Fund' and moved in August 1979 by road to Steamport Transport Museum. Unusually, it was hauled onto its low-loader trailer by a veteran Sentinel steam tractor. With little restoration work having been carried out – and following the closure of the Steamport Transport Museum and removal of stock to the new Ribble Steam Railway at Preston Docks – No 5193 was purchased by the WSR Company, moving to Minehead on 2 December 1998.

At the Annual General Meeting of WSR plc in June 2000, it was formally announced that an ambitious plan had been drawn up to convert No 5193 from a 2-6-2T into a 2-6-0 tender locomotive. There were several reasons behind this. First, it was felt that in the new form, the locomotive would offer greater operational flexibility with its larger coal and Water capacity. Second, on examination of the locomotive it was found that the coal bunker and side tanks were beyond economic repair. Also, the rear drag box and frames were badly wasted, which would necessitate total replacement. The modified locomotive would require a tender, new cab, modified drag box, and splashers. The concept was not new – both G. J. Churchward and C. B. Collett had considered a similar scheme while in office as a means of providing a lighter version of the '43xx'/'93xx' Class. When rebuilt, the new 'Mogul' would have a boiler 5½ inches lower and a firebox 6 inches lower than a '43xx' 2-6-0, the cab

Seen backing away from the buffer stops at Minehead, the clean lines of No 9351 are much admired by many enthusiasts and this locomotive has proved to be a valuable addition to the fleet. *M. J. Stretton*

would have side windows and the lever reverse would be retained. Other changes would include different springs and a front running plate curve.

The new millennium marked the start in earnest of the rebuild at Minehead, with the locomotive stripped down; by the close of 2001 work was well advanced on refitting the motion and other parts onto the shortened frames. In 2004 the number 9351 was chosen for the new locomotive – an appropriate choice for the first member of a new class and, interestingly, also an anagram of the original.

A major landmark was achieved on 2 September 2004 when the almost complete locomotive was moved out of Minehead shed and the fire lit pending a visit from the boiler inspector. All that remained was the cosmetic work and full painting (in unlined GWR green), the locomotive being introduced on service trains during the 2004 Autumn Steam Gala. No 9351 has also now joined the list of WSR locomotives that have worked on other heritage railways, making a brief visit to the Severn Valley Railway for its Autumn Steam Gala in September 2005.

No 9351 settled down into regular service on the WSR and has already run in excess of 20,000 miles since entering traffic. Withdrawn on the expiry of its ten-year boiler certificate in mid-2015, it has recently undergone an overhaul in Minehead, returning to service on the WSR in 2016.

| | |
|---|---|
| Tractive effort | 24,300lb |
| Boiler pressure | 200lbs/sq in |
| Power class | D |
| Route availability | Blue |
| Locomotive weight (in full working order) | 61t 5cwt |
| Tender weight (in full working order) | 40t 0cwt |
| Tender weight (empty) | 18t 15cwt |
| Length(tender) | 24ft 4½ins |
| Total wheelbase | 58ft 1ins |
| Coupled wheelbase | 14ft 9ins |
| Width | 8ft 11ins |
| Height | 12ft 11½ins |
| Wheel diameter (pony truck) | 3ft 2ins |
| Wheel diameter (driving) | 5ft 8ins |

| | |
|---|---|
| Wheel diameter (tender) | 4ft 1½ins |
| Boiler diameter | 4ft 5½ins |
| Number of tubes | 218 |
| Length of tubes | 12ft 0ins |
| Tube heating surface | 1,145 sq ft |
| Grate area | 20.3 sq ft |
| Firebox surface area | 121 sq ft |
| Number of flues | 6 |
| Superheater surface area | 82 sq ft |
| Cylinders | 18ins x 30ins (2 Outside) |
| Valve gear | Stephenson (Inside) |
| Coal capacity | 6t |
| Water capacity | 3,500 gallons |
| Maximum axle load | 17t 12cwt |

# 44422

## LMSR 0-6-0 (LMS No 4422)

Built at the Derby Locomotive Works of the London Midland & Scottish Railway to a design by Sir Henry Fowler, No 4422 was classified as a superheated freight locomotive with a 4F power rating. Construction of the class had started in 1911 by the Midland Railway, and a total of 772 were built, our example being completed in October 1927 at a cost of £3,217 plus an additional £1,000 for the tender. Records show that its first shed allocation was Leicester, with a subsequent transfer to Wigston in January 1929. In 1940 it moved to Bristol, where it became a West Country locomotive for the rest of its revenue-earning life, with a further move the few miles to Bath Green Park shed in 1948. Nationalisation saw No 4422 become No 44422, and it established itself as a regular performer over the former Somerset & Dorset Railway route piloting holiday specials, perhaps even with No 53808 (see below).

### Time Line

**Built:** October 1927
Derby Works

**Known shed allocations:**
1927 Leicester
1929 Wigston
1940 Bristol
1948 Bath Green Park
1960 Templecombe
1965 Gloucester

**Withdrawn:** June 1965

**Rescued:** May 1977

**Arrival at WSR:** tbc

No 44422 is seen in the company of No 53809 at Nethercott bridge. *Don Bishop*

During 1952 No 44422 was sent to Horwich Works for overhaul – an event that was to be its last in BR service – returning to the West after a period of running-in. It was then transferred to Templecombe in November 1960, finally being withdrawn from Gloucester shed in June 1965. It was sent to Barry, arriving in August and staying there until April 1977, when it was purchased for preservation by North Staffordshire Railway Society members from Cheddleton. At a cost of £4,860, it was the 87th locomotive to leave Barry, and steamed again in preservation at Cheddleton in September 1990. Four of the class have been preserved, and ours is the only left-hand-drive example.

Now owned by the 44422 Locomotive Company Ltd, and re-entering traffic after a further major overhaul, it was put on general hire visiting many preserved railways, including the West Somerset Railway in 2006 and 2007. Withdrawn again from service in 2013 at the Nene Valley Railway, Peak Rail allowed it to be stored at Rowsley. An agreement was then signed with the WSR for a 25-year period. The boiler having been sent to Crewe, the locomotive returned to traffic in time for the railway's Spring Steam Gala in March 2016, the theme being to commemorate the Somerset & Dorset Railway. No 44422 is paired with tender No 3978, built in 1928, formerly belonging to LMS 'Crab' 2-6-0 No 2763.

| | |
|---|---|
| Tractive effort | 24,555lb |
| Boiler pressure | 175lbs/sq in |
| Power class | 4F |
| Route availability | 5 |
| Locomotive weight (in full working order) | 48t 15cwt |
| Tender weight (in full working order) | 42t 2cwt |
| Tender weight (empty) | 21t 6cwt |
| Length (tender) | tbc |
| Total length | 52ft 0ins |
| Coupled wheelbase | tbc |
| Width | 8ft 11ins |
| Height | 13ft 2½ins |

| | |
|---|---|
| Wheel diameter (driving) | 5ft 3ins |
| Wheel diameter (tender) | 4ft 3ins |
| Length of tubes | 11ft 11ins |
| Tube heating surface | 1,034 sq ft |
| Grate area | 21 sq ft |
| Firebox surface area | 151 sq ft |
| Cylinders | 20ins x 26ins (2 inside) |
| Valve gear | Stephenson (Inside) |
| Coal capacity | 5t 10cwt |
| Water capacity | 3,500 gallons |

# 53808 S&DJR 2-8-0 (LMS Nos 9678, 13808)

This class dates from 1914 when Henry (later Sir Henry) Fowler at Derby produced designs for a type of a locomotive hitherto unknown on the Midland Railway, incorporating such features as Walschaerts valve gear and outside cylinders. The locomotives were built in two batches, the first six (S&DJR Nos 80-85) arriving at Bath in 1914, followed by Nos 86-90 in 1925. They were specifically provided to work the Somerset & Dorset line between Bournemouth and Bath, jointly leased by the London & South Western Railway and the Midland Railway, the latter assuming responsibility for the provision of motive power.

The WSR-based 7F is one of the later batch, built by the Darlington Works of Robert Stephenson & Co in 1925 as S&D No 88. It was turned out in unlined black livery, to works order No 3894, at a cost of £6,570. When built it had a larger-diameter boiler (5ft 3in) than is evident on the locomotive today, the change having occurred in 1953 as part of a general repair, when the boiler was declared unfit. However, as the locomotive still had a few years life left, a temporary solution was found by re-boilering the 7Fs with 4ft 9in

## Time Line

**Built:** October 1925
Robert Stephenson & Co
Derby Works

**Known shed allocations:**
1925 Bath Green Park

**Withdrawn:** March 1964

**Rescued:** May 1970

**Arrival at WSR:** Early 2016

Seen at Minehead in the livery of the Somerset & Dorset Joint Railway and carrying the number 88 this fine locomotive is due to re-enter traffic during 2016 following its latest 10-year overhaul. *Keith Smith*

boilers removed from withdrawn 'Compounds' at Derby. No 53808 received the boiler from No 41092.

Unusually – certainly as far as the other WSR-based locomotives are concerned – the 2-8-0 spent the whole of its working life based at one shed, Bath Green Park. It mainly worked the local goods trains between Bath and Evercreech Junction, which involved a stiff climb over the Mendip Hills in both directions, although in the post-war period it was also used to haul some of the many Summer Saturday holiday trains to and from the North. The ability of the 7Fs to haul these heavy trains unassisted made them a popular choice for this work. Only rarely did No 88 venture up the branch from Evercreech Junction to Highbridge and Glastonbury. The daily routine of working over Somerset & Dorset metals was broken only by visits to Derby Works for repair, as well as occasional trips up the Midland main line from Bath to Westerleigh Yard, north of Mangotsfield. No 53808 was also a popular choice for rail tours in its latter years.

This evocative black and white image shows the locomotive carrying the BR number 53808 and the lined black livery in whch it will be seen on its return to regular service. *Keith Smith*

In 1926-27 No 88 featured in dynamometer car tests on the Toton-Brent coal trains with two LNWR 0-8-0s, and again in 1930 between Bath and Wellow. In 1930, when S&DJR locomotives were taken into LMS stock, No 88 became No 9678. It was renumbered again in 1932 as No 13808, and upon nationalisation of the railways in 1948 it became British Railways No 53808.

No 53808 was finally withdrawn from active service in March 1964, and was subsequently deposited – together with No 53809 – in Barry scrapyard, where it arrived in June 1964. The Somerset & Dorset Railway Circle (later Trust) decided to raise funds to purchase the locomotive in late 1968. This appeal was successful, and the 2-8-0 was hauled dead from Barry to Bristol on 3 October 1970, where it appeared at the Bath Road Diesel Depot Open Day two weeks later. It was then moved, again by rail, to Radstock, where the S&DRT was establishing a restoration base. Work progressed on the 7F as funds permitted, but following the collapse of the Radstock project the S&DRT successfully concluded arrangements for its stock to be moved to the West Somerset Railway, arriving on the line on 9 January 1976.

The S&DRT established a new base at Washford station, No 53808 finally arriving there on 18 December 1977. Restoration progressed steadily but, because of the Trust's commitments to other projects, become very prolonged, and in April 1985 the decision was made to place the restoration of the 2-8-0 out to contract. Negotiations were successfully concluded with WSR plc, which initially undertook the work on site at Washford, dealing mainly with the frames and motion. The frames were rewheeled at Washford on 21 January 1986, and nine days later No D2271 moved the rolling chassis to Minehead for the restoration to be completed. The boiler was returned to the frames on 22 February 1987.

The locomotive, initially painted in unlined black livery with the early BR crest, and bearing the number 53808, returned to steam on 19 August 1987 in time to celebrate 125 years of the Somerset & Dorset Railway. It quickly became a 'regular' in the WSR steam fleet. During the spring of 1992 the locomotive was painted in non-authentic black livery as S&DJR No 88, and was again repainted into BR unlined black (with the later crest) as No 53808 in early 1996, in time for the WSR's 'Somerset & Dorset Anniversary Gala' in March of that year. During this time it left the railway for a brief spell during September-October 1995 to 'guest' on the Severn Valley Railway.

No 53808 was withdrawn from service in May 1996 for its ten-year overhaul, after working almost 50,000 miles in service on the WSR. The work was largely carried out at Minehead, with the boiler being sent away for a contract repair. The work on the frames included the casting, machining and fitting of

| | |
|---|---|
| Tractive effort | 35,296lb |
| Boiler pressure | 190lbs/sq in |
| Power class | 7F |
| Locomotive weight (in full working order) | 64t 15cwt |
| Tender weight (in full working order) | 40t 0cwt |
| Total length | 59ft 10ins |
| Total wheelbase | 49ft 4ins |
| Coupled wheelbase | 17ft 6ins |
| Width | 8ft 11ins |
| Height | 13ft 2½ins |
| Wheel diameter (pony truck) | 3ft 3½ins |
| Wheel diameter (driving) | 4ft 7½ins |
| Wheel diameter (tender) | 4ft 3ins |
| Boiler diameter | 4ft 8ins |

| | |
|---|---|
| Number of tubes | 169 |
| Length of tubes | 11ft 11ins |
| Tube heating surface | 1,170 sq ft |
| Grate area | 28.4 sq ft |
| Firebox surface area | 148 sq ft |
| Number of flues | 27 |
| Superheater surface area | 374 sq ft |
| Cylinders | 21ins x 28ins (2 Outside) |
| Valve gear | Walschaerts (Outside) |
| Coal capacity | 5½t |
| Water capacity | 3,500 gallons |
| Maximum axle load | 16t 0cwt |

completely new cylinder blocks, due to the originals being beyond economic repair. The boiler was almost new when it was returned to Minehead on 1 December 2004 – the firebox, for example, was completely renewed – making it probably the most extensive boiler overhaul in railway preservation.

After final reassembly, No 88 returned to steam in October 2005 – painted in S&D Prussian blue (a livery previously only used on S&D passenger engines) – and performed regular duties on the WSR. Taken out of service again for a further ten-yearly overhaul in 2015, the locomotive returned to service for the 50th anniversary of the closure of the Somerset & Dorset Railway in March 2016, but this time in its original unlined black BR livery as No 53808.

# Former industrial steam locomotives

## 1788 Peckett 0-4-0ST *Kilmersdon*

No 1788 is seen here rather resplendent, although not strictly accurate, in the colours of the SDJR. *Keith Smith*

### Time Line

**Built:** October 1929
Atlas Works, Bristol

**Known shed allocations:**
1929 Kilmersdon Colliery

**Withdrawn:** c1973

**Rescued:** c1974

**Arrival at WSR:** May 1975

This locomotive, one of many, was built at the Atlas Locomotive Works, Bristol, of Messrs Peckett & Sons Limited. It worked regularly at the various collieries around Radstock in Somerset, several of which were linked to the Somerset & Dorset line between Bath and Bournemouth. Its duties were mundane, but very essential to the efficient operation of the collieries.

When the last two collieries in the Radstock area

(Writhlington and Kilmersdon) finally closed for good on 30 September 1973, *Kilmersdon* became the last steam locomotive to work in a Somerset coalfield. The National Coal Board subsequently placed the 0-4-0ST under the care of the Somerset & Dorset Railway Trust. Prior to moving to the Trust's first base at Radstock, the locomotive gave trips at Radstock Colliery by arrangement with the NCB, but it was then moved by road – still in light steam – to the Camerton Traction Engine Rally. A further road movement brought the locomotive to Bishops Lydeard station on the WSR in May 1975. *Kilmersdon* was eventually transferred by rail to Washford, the new (and current) home of the S&DRT, to be put on display.

In 1988 the decision was made for the 0-4-0ST to receive a thorough overhaul and, with the aid of a generous grant from the NCB, was sent to the Midland Railway Centre at Butterley for this to be carried out. The work was completed in mid-1991 and, after travelling under its own steam from Bishops Lydeard to Washford, *Kilmersdon* was formally recommissioned on 17-18 August 1991.

The Peckett tank is too light to be used on WSR passenger trains, but in recent years it has become a regular and popular star at the railway's 'Friends of Thomas the Tank Engine' events, where it masquerades as No 6 *Percy*. The locomotive has also been used on 'Steam Engineman' courses. When not in use, No 1788 is kept and maintained by the S&DRT at Washford.

August 2001 saw the expiry of the engine's ten-year boiler certificate, resulting in the routine withdrawal from service, and it was temporarily removed from the railway on 17 October that year to a private site in Taunton, where members of 5542 Limited undertook the overhaul. Now back in active service, and painted in a replica of the S&DJR livery, the locomotive is steamed at Washford during Gala and other special events.

| | |
|---|---|
| Tractive effort | 10,680lb |
| Boiler pressure | 160lb/sq in |
| Length | 21ft 4in |
| Height | 10ft 2in |
| Wheel diameter | 3ft 0in |
| Number of tubes | 96 |
| Tube heating surface | 392 sq ft |
| Grate area | 5.25 sq ft |
| Cylinders (2, outside) | 12in x 20in |

# 1219 Andrew Barclay 0-4-0ST

No 1219 was taken out of Williton works specially for this image to be taken – thanks to one and all, especially in view of the inclement weather! *Duncan Hensley*

## Time Line

**Built:** January 1911
Andrew Barclay Sons & Co. Caledonia Works, Kilmarnock

**Known shed allocations:**
1911 Stewart & Lloyds Mossend
19?? Andrew Barclay Sons & Co. Caledonia Works, Kilmarnock

**Withdrawn:** 1970

**Rescued:** 1August 1970

**Arrival at WSR:** 2012

Completed at the Caledonia Works of Andrew Barclay Sons & Co Ltd at Kilmarnock on 17 January 1911, the locomotive was delivered new to the Clydesdale Works of Stewarts & Lloyds at Mossend, becoming that company's No 9. At some point the locomotive was sold back to Barclay, where it become employed as works shunter. It was ultimately sold into preservation in August 1970, then on to an apprentice at West Somerset Restorations in Williton. Arriving from the South Cambridgeshire Steam Museum on 26 April 2012, restoration was completed by early 2016, and the 0-4-0ST will run in the Caledonia Works livery. It is mainly intended to be a hired-out locomotive when not used for demonstrations and special occasions.

| | |
|---|---|
| Boiler pressure | 160lb/sq in |
| Wheel diameter | 3ft 0in |
| Number of tubes | 96 |
| Cylinders (2, outside) | 10in x 18in |
| Valve gear | Stephenson (inside) |

# Former main-line diesel locomotives

## D1010 'Western' Class 52 C-C

*Western Campaigner*

### Time Line

**Built:** October 1962
Swindon Works

**Known shed allocations:**
1962 Old Oak Common
1964 Plymouth Laira
1968 Swansea Landore
1968 Plymouth Laira

**Withdrawn:** February 1977

**Rescued:** July 1977

**Arrival at WSR:** 1991

The Type 4 'Westerns', later Class 52, were introduced in 1961 by British Railways, Western Region. Every one of the 74 built were based and worked on the Region, and carried a 'Western' name. They were equipped with hydraulic transmission in company with other WR classes, compared with the electric transmission of other BR main-line diesel locomotives. Because they were deemed non-standard, forming only 11 per cent of the entire BR diesel fleet, hydraulic locomotives were gradually withdrawn from service, the 'Western' Class being the last to go. In their later days, all were based at Plymouth Laira depot, handling the principal expresses between London Paddington, Plymouth and Penzance. It is therefore very appropriate that a member of the class is preserved, and in use in the South West. The locomotives were a regular sight at Taunton, but were considered too heavy at the time for use on the Minehead branch.

No D1010 was completed at Swindon in October 1962 under Lot 450, and was immediately allocated to Old Oak Common depot. The livery on entering service was maroon – the first Swindon-built 'Western' to be so painted – but this soon changed to BR 'all over' blue with full yellow front ends. Subsequent allocations were Plymouth Laira (January 1964), Swansea Landore (January 1968), and back to Plymouth Laira (November 1968).

*Opposite page:* No 1010 *Western Campaigner* is seen at Kentsford Crossing on 20 July 2013. *Kelvin Lumb*

*Above:* No D1010 *Western Campaigner* in full flight! *Keith Smith*

*Western Campaigner* became renowned for being a fast runner, and held some of the best 'Western' timings. The locomotive returned to Swindon for its last overhaul, an Intermediate, in July 1972, during which dual-brake equipment was fitted. It achieved a connection with the WSR on 17 March 1975, when it towed the LMS 'Pacific' No 6229 *Duchess of Hamilton* from Taunton to Swindon, following the steam locomotive's time on display at Butlin's Holiday Camp at Minehead. The locomotive was finally withdrawn from Plymouth Laira in February 1977, after running 1,360,000 miles, and was placed in store at Newton Abbot.

While there No D1010 was purchased for preservation by Foster Yeoman, the quarry company, which moved it to its Merehead works in East Somerset on 6 July 1977. To highlight the 'Yeoman connection', on 15 July 1984 the locomotive appeared as the previously scrapped No D1035 *Western Yeoman* in green livery, with non-authentic yellow ends. In May 1985 No D1035 was loaned to the Diesel & Electric Preservation Group for restoration at Didcot. After a few years in action at Didcot, courtesy of the Great Western Society, the D&EPG decided in 1990 to concentrate its locomotives on the WSR. Following tyre-turning at Cardiff Canton, *Western Yeoman* was towed by rail to Norton Fitzwarren on 11 January 1991 where, upon arrival, it ran under its own power to Williton, the D&EPG's base on the line. The 'Western' entered service on the WSR at the Spring Diesel Gala in March 1991, operating on one engine only and running in 'desert sand' livery, which had been carried for several years by the prototype No D1000 *Western Enterprise*. However, this was soon to be changed to BR green, complete with small yellow end panels. In addition to its work on the West Somerset, No D1035 has also become a well-travelled locomotive, working on the Paignton & Dartmouth

Railway in mid-June 1991, followed by a number of appearances at BR Open Days at Bristol Bath Road, Gloucester and Laira, followed by service on the Bodmin & Wenford Railway. By March 1992 both engines were operational but, in the autumn of that year, the locomotive was withdrawn for major work following its purchase by the D&EPG from Foster Yeoman. It re-entered service as No D1010 *Western Campaigner* for the WSR Autumn Diesel Gala carrying the British Railways Corporate Blue livery.

During 1995 and 1996 the locomotive was withdrawn from service again so that further work could be undertaken to improve its reliability in service. Tasks undertaken included a partial rewire and attention to the two Maybach MD655 engines. After re-entering service again in 1996, and having completed a further 4,000 miles, another withdrawal took place at the end of 2000, this time because of an oil leak in one of the Voith transmission units. For the 2001 season the locomotive appeared from winter hibernation in a new maroon livery with no yellow warning panels, and completed 940 miles in WSR service. *Western Campaigner*'s next appearance was for the 2002 May Gala, but was stopped afterwards for attention to a heat exchanger. While stopped, a minor change was made to the livery with the addition of small yellow cab-front warning panels. It re-entered service again for the Somerset CAMRA Real Ale Festival in September 2002. In 2003 No D1010 completed 1,148 miles in 13 trouble-free service days, its highest annual mileage in preservation. Appearing again in 2004, the locomotive only managed to run 220 service miles before withdrawal with transmission reverser problems, and an increasing oil leak from the transmission. Due to other commitments, *Western Campaigner* was stored until May 2005, when a start was finally made on preparing to remove the troublesome transmission unit. The 'Western' is used during special events, and occasionally in the peak months when heritage diesel locomotives work the DMU diagram.

| | |
|---|---|
| Wheel configuration | C-C |
| Wheel diameter | 3ft 7ins |
| Length | 68ft 0ins |
| Width | 8ft 8ins |
| Height | 12ft 11¾ins |
| Weight | 108t |
| Fuel capacity | 850 gallons |
| Engines | Maybach MD655 (x2) |
| Power output | 1,380bhp @ 1500rpm |
| Maximum speed | 90mph |
| Tractive effort | Maximum 66700lbs, continuous 45,200lbs @ 14.5mph |
| Transmission | Voith L630rU |
| Route availability | 7 |
| BR power rating | 4 |

# D1661

## Class 47 Co-Co
*North Star*

These Type 4 diesel-electrics, later Class 47, were introduced between 1963 and 1967, and our example entered service on 13 February 1965. Originally numbered D1661, and based at Cardiff Canton, it received the name *North Star* in March 1965 at Paddington, before hauling a special train to Bristol. Although the name was maintained throughout the locomotive's working life, the number changed several times, to 47077 in March 1974, 47613 in March 1984, and 47840 in November 1989. *North Star*'s livery has also changed, starting with dual green, BR blue, InterCity, Virgin, BR blue again, and finally back to dual green in preservation. It should also be noted that, while in BR blue, the 'large logo' was never applied.

The locomotive eventually become part of the cross-country fleet after being converted from a Class 47/4 to a Class 47/8 with the fitting of long-range fuel tanks to enable longer runs between refuelling stops. During this period, and as part of the Virgin fleet, it hauled the last regular Virgin cross-country Class 47-hauled service from Penzance to Birmingham New Street on 19 August 2002; it was for this occasion that the BR blue livery was reapplied. After this, D1661 was retained for 'Thunderbird' train-rescue duties and weekend work assisting electric-hauled services on non-electrified diversions because of engineering work. After Virgin acquired the Class 57 locomotives

### Time Line

**Built:** February 1965
Brush Works Loughborough

**Known shed allocations:**
1965 Cardiff Canton
1984 Old Oak Common
1988 Bristol Bath Road
1989 Crewe
1992 Bristol Bath Road
1995 Tinsley
1995 Bristol Bath Road
1995 Crewe
1998 Toton
2004 Willesden
2005 Plymouth Laira
2005 Old Oak Common (Stored)
2006 Gloucester Horton Road
2007 Old Oak Common

**Withdrawn:** 2007

**Rescued:** 2007

**Arrival at WSR:** May 2007

Looking impressive in BR two-tone green livery, No D1661 *North Star* provides a powerful workhorse on the WSR. *Keith Smith*

| | |
|---|---|
| Wheel configuration | Co-Co |
| Wheel diameter | 3ft 9ins |
| Length | 63ft 7ins |
| Width | 8ft 10ins |
| Height | 12ft 9½ins |
| Weight | 124t |
| Fuel capacity | 1,295 gallons |
| Engines | Sulzer 12LDA28-C |
| Power output | 2,580bhp |
| Maximum speed | 95mph |
| Tractive effort | Maximum 60,000lbs |
| Transmission | Brush traction motors |
| Route availability | 6 or 7 |
| BR power rating | 4 |

for this purpose, *North Star* was moved to the Alstom pool at Willesden in August 2004, but the following April made the short trip over to Old Oak Common to work for First Great Western on sleeper shunt release duties at Paddington.

Since 1995 the Class 47 had been transferred to Porterbrook Leasing, and when this ended ownership was transferred to the D&EPG. Running under train reporting number 0Z47, it ran light engine from Old Oak Common to Brush Traction at Loughborough for a repaint into the green livery now carried. *North Star* hauled a rail tour from Derby on Bank Holiday Monday, 28 May 2007, and on arrival at Minehead a formal hand-over ceremony took place.

## D2133 Class 03 0-6-0DM

Resting in the sun at Minehead is station pilot No D2133 *Keith Smith*

### Time Line

**Built:** October 1960
Swindon Works

**Known shed allocations:**
1960 Taunton
1969 Courtaulds Bridgwater

**Withdrawn:** 1994

**Rescued:** May 1994

**Arrival at WSR:** 1994

The railway's Class 03 shunter is very much a 'local engine'. No D2133 was built by BR at Swindon in 1960 and has the standard-height cab. It was supplied new to Taunton shed, performing local shunting duties around the various yards, but it was also recorded working further away at Highbridge and Bridgwater. Evidence also exists of No D2133 working demolition trains on the Somerset & Dorset line after its closure in 1966.

With local goods traffic, for which the class was designed, rapidly diminishing in the Taunton area, the '03' was withdrawn by BR and subsequently purchased by Courtaulds Film Cellophane in 1969 for use at its Bridgwater works. It was used regularly on shunting duties at the factory – which for many years was rail-connected – until being taken out of service in 1994.

The locomotive was then kindly donated to WSR plc – a plaque on the bodyside recognising this generosity – and it is usually deployed as station pilot at Minehead, though it, too, has worked passenger shuttle services at special events. No D2133 carries the early BR green livery, complete with 'wasp ends'.

| | |
|---|---|
| Wheel configuration | 0-6-0 |
| Wheel diameter | 3ft 7ins |
| Length | 26ft 0ins |
| Width | 8ft 6ins |
| Height | 12ft 27/16 ins |
| Weight | 30.2t |
| Fuel capacity | 510 gallons |
| Engines | Gardner 8L3 |
| Power output | 204bhp |

| | |
|---|---|
| Maximum speed | 28.5mph |
| Tractive effort | Maximum 15,650lbs |
| Wheelbase | 9ft 0ins |
| Transmission | Wilson Drewry CA5R7 5-speed epicycle gearbox, RF11 spiral bevel reverse and final drive |

## D2271 Class 04 0-6-0DM

The other diesel shunter based on the line, this Class 04 was built in 1958 as Drewry Car Company No DC2615 by Robert Stephenson & Hawthorn (Works No RSH7913). It was in service with British Railways until withdrawn from Bradford Hammerton Street shed (55F) on 26 October 1969, and was subsequently sold into industrial

No D2271 on a works train. *Terry Gough*

### Time Line

**Built:** 1958 Robert Stephenson & Hawthorn

**Known shed allocations:** Bradford Hamerton Street

**Withdrawn:** 1969

**Rescued:** 1975

**Arrival at WSR:** 1982

use, moving to C. F. Booth Ltd of Rotherham. It was sold again on 18 July 1972, and put into store for a year at Thomas Hill Ltd, Rotherham, followed by a further 21 months at Normanton Barracks, Derby.

In May 1975 No D2271 entered preservation and was moved to the Midland Railway Centre at Butterley, Derbyshire, before being transferred to the WSR in May 1982. After gearbox repairs, the locomotive was put into service on engineering trains, but has since become the regular station pilot at Minehead, appearing in a non-authentic blue livery.

| | |
|---|---|
| Wheel configuration | 0-6-0 |
| Wheel diameter | 3ft 6in |
| Length | 26ft 0in |
| Width | 8ft 6in |
| Height | 12ft 1½in |
| Weight | 30.2 tons |
| Fuel capacity | 225 gallons |
| Engine | Gardner 8L3 |
| Power output | 204hp |

| | |
|---|---|
| Maximum speed | 27mph |
| Tractive effort | Maximum 15,650lbf |
| Wheelbase | 9ft 0in |
| Transmission | Wilson Drewry CA5R7 five-speed epicycle gearbox, RF11 spiral bevel reverse and final drive |

## D4107 Class 09 0-6-0DE (also BR No 09019)

The Class 09 diesel shunters were a variation of the successful Class 08s, the only difference being that they were geared to give a maximum speed of 27mph for trip working as opposed to the Class 08's maximum speed of 15-20mph. This resulted in the Class 09 having a lower

No D4107 is another handy workhorse and dates from 1961. *WSR Collection*

### Time Line

**Built:** December 1961 Horwich Works

**Known shed allocations:**
1961 Carlisle Upperby
1968 Hither Green
2010 Toton

**Withdrawn:** 2010

**Rescued:** 2013

**Arrival at WSR:** 2013

power output of 25000lbf TE, whereas the 08s' TE was 35,000lbf.

Our example was built at Horwich in December 1961, and its first shed allocation was Carlisle Upperby, but it moved south to Hither Green in October 1968. In 1973 it was renumbered 09019. During the British Rail privatisation process, No 09019 was allocated to Mainline Freight and painted in that company's blue livery. Withdrawn from Toton in June 2010 and sold to HNRC, it was moved to Nemesis Rail at Burton-on-Trent. Now owned by 4160 Ltd, the shunter arrived on the WSR on 6 March 2013, and was painted in its original green livery as No D4107 at Washford in November 2014. It is usually seen at Bishops Lydeard, where it is the resident station pilot.

| | |
|---|---|
| Wheel configuration | 0-6-0 |
| Wheel diameter | 4ft 6ins |
| Length | 29ft 3ins |
| Width | 8ft 6ins |
| Height | 12ft 8½in |
| Weight | 30.2t |
| Fuel capacity | 510 gallons |
| Engines | English Electric 400hp 6KT |
| Traction motors | 2 x English Electric 506 |
| Power output | 350bhp |
| Maximum speed | 27mph |
| Tractive effort | Maximum 25,000lbs |
| Wheelbase | 11ft 6ins |

## D6566 Class 33 Bo-Bo (also BR No 33048)

Built by the Birmingham Railway Carriage & Wagon Company at Smethwick, the Sulzer Type 3s – later Class 33 and nicknamed 'Cromptons' – were built in 1961-62 for use on the Southern Region of British Railways. A total of 98 locomotives were built, Nos D6500-D6597, weighing 78 tons, fitted with a Sulzer 8LDA28A engine, and having a Maximum speed of 85mph. The locomotives were subsequently formed into three sub-classes, 33/0, 33/1 and 33/2.

When new, the livery carried was standard BR Brunswick Green with a light grey band at mid-height and white window surrounds. Buffer beams were red and the roof was grey, with black bogies and running gear. Later, yellow panels were included on the ends, but they were replaced by full yellow ends from the mid-1960s. After 1967 'Rail Blue' became the standard colour scheme for the class, before the 'sectorisation'

### Time Line

**Built:** 1961
BRCWC Works, Smethwick

**Known shed allocations:**
1961 Hither Green

**Withdrawn:**
1995 (active service)
1997 (from Training Loco)

**Rescued:** 1997

**Arrival at WSR:** 1997

of BR brought their own individual colours from the late 1980s. In the later years of BR the Class 33s could also be seen in action on the Western Region. While the majority of the class have now been withdrawn, a small number are still main-line certificated.

No D6566, built in 1961, spent its entire life based on the Southern Region, working both passenger and freight trains. It was renumbered 33048 in the mid-1970s under the TOPS scheme. After its withdrawal by BR in 1995, the locomotive spent two years in store at Hither Green, where it was used for staff training purposes It was then purchased privately, and moved to the WSR in May 1997. In remarkably good condition, and with only 30 components missing, the engine was started up after just two months' work at Williton by volunteer members of the Diesel & Electric Preservation Group. After a number of test runs were successfully undertaken, No 33048 made its WSR passenger debut at a Diesel Running Day held on 25 October 1997.

The 'Crompton' – privately owned, and operated under a Locomotive Management Agreement by the D&EPG – has subsequently settled down to become a regular and consistent member of the operational fleet, working more than 11,000 miles in service on the WSR to date. Much of this has been achieved working trains for the Civil Engineer and the Signal & Telegraph Department, and stock moves in support of the steam fleet. To mark its 40th anniversary, the '33' was given a light body overhaul and repaint, again in 'all-over blue', but a full repaint in its original green livery has now taken place.

Low-loaders are used to transport locomotives by road as seen here with No D6566 on the move. *Keith Smith*

| | |
|---|---|
| Wheel configuration | Bo-Bo |
| Wheel diameter | 3ft 7ins |
| Length | 50ft 9ins |
| Width | 8ft 10ins |
| Height | 12ft 8 in |
| Weight | 78t |
| Fuel capacity | 800 gallons |
| Engines | Sulzer 8LDA28 |
| Transmission | DC traction motors (x4) |
| Power output | 1,550bhp |
| Maximum speed | 85mph |
| Tractive effort | Maximum 45,000lbs continuous 26,000lbs |
| Route availability | 6 |
| BR power rating | 3 |

# D6575 Class 33 Bo-Bo (also BR No 33057 *Seagull*)

The locomotives on the WSR are cleaned and polished regularly and No D6575 is a gleaming example in this shot! *Keith Smith*

## Time Line

**Built:** 1961
BRCWC Works, Smethwick

**Known shed allocations:**
1961 Hither Green
1985 Stewarts Lane
1990 Eastleigh
19?? Stewarts Lane

**Withdrawn:** 1997

**Rescued:** 2005

**Arrival at WSR:** 2005

The second 'Crompton' to be based on the West Somerset Railway was also built by the Birmingham Railway Carriage & Wagon Company (Works No DEL179). It entered service in November 1961 and was initially allocated to Hither Green depot, being reallocated to Stewarts Lane in November 1985. After the locomotive received a heavy overhaul at Eastleigh Works in May 1990, Eastleigh became its home depot until it was reallocated back to Stewarts Lane and subsequent withdrawal in February 1997. It was given the name *Seagull* in May 1991.

After a period in store at the Ministry of Defence site at Smallstown, No 33057 was purchased by Direct Rail Services, with the intention of overhauling it and returning it to use on freight services, including nuclear flask trains. However, a change in policy resulted in the loco being put up for sale, and it was purchased privately and delivered by road to the WSR in mid-summer 2005. Although initially intended to be no more than a parts donor locomotive to keep D6566 in working order, it was decided that D6575 should be returned to traffic in its own right. As a result, the locomotive was sent to the East Somerset Railway for extensive bodywork repairs, returning on 16 June 2015. Further mechanical overhaul took place at Williton to bring the locomotive into working order.

Technical details for D6575 are as for D6566 on page 42.

# D7017 'Hymek' Class 35 B-B

*Above and below:* One of two Hymeks on the WSR at the time of writing No D7017 is seen at Blue Anchor and at Stogumber. *Keith Smith/Kelvin Lumb*

## Time Line

**Built:** January 1962
Beyer Peacock

**Known shed allocations:**
1962 Bristol Bath Road
1971 Old Oak Common

**Withdrawn:** March 1975

**Rescued:** May 1975

**Arrival at WSR:** 1975

Unlike the other Regions of British Railways, the Western Region carried on the GWR tradition of individuality by replacing its steam locomotives with diesel locomotives incorporating hydraulic, rather than electric, transmission in the early 1960s. The largest class of diesel-hydraulics introduced were the Type 3s (later Class 35) commonly known as 'Hymeks' – so named after Beyer-Peacock (Hymek) Ltd, which manufactured the Mekydro hydraulic/mechanical transmission used on the locomotives. The 'Hymeks' were primarily designed to work passenger trains throughout the Western Region but, particularly in later years, also appeared on other duties including parcels and freight turns.

No D7017 was one of the initial order of 45 locomotives costing £80,000 each, and as Beyer-Peacock No 7911 under Lot 449 was delivered early in 1962. It was allocated to the new diesel maintenance depot at Bristol Bath Road, where it remained until being reallocated to Old Oak Common in October 1971. It was withdrawn from

service in May 1973, only to be reinstated – together with nine other members of the class – shortly after to help with the summer traffic. However, by mid-1974 only three 'Hymeks' remained in service, and soon only two, Nos D7017 and D7018, were active. The former was finally withdrawn on 13 March 1975.

By this time a society, the Diesel & Electric Group, had been formed, and its main interest was in diesel and electric traction. It was actively attempting to preserve a main-line diesel locomotive, and after unsuccessfully tendering for No D7022, eventually purchased D7017 in May 1975. Under 13 years of BR ownership the locomotive had covered some 655,000 miles, had carried nine different engines, seven different hydraulic transmissions, and seven pairs of bogies. On 30 June 1975 the locomotive left London for the last time towed behind Class 25 No 25162, destined for Taunton and eventual preservation on the West Somerset Railway, where the Group had decided to focus its activities.

No D7017 is based at the D&EPG's centre at Williton, where the Group had established a restoration and maintenance depot. Originally restored in its former BR two-tone green livery, it was temporarily painted in the grey and yellow engineers' livery and carried the number 35017 for the WSR 1992 Autumn Diesel Gala, although it never carried these colours when in service with BR. Following this event, the 'Hymek' was repainted again in full BR 'all-over blue' livery with full yellow ends, and reverted to being No D7017. During 1993 it was repainted again, receiving small yellow end panels and white cab window frames. At the same time, a new heat exchanger and replacement air compressor were installed, ready for an appearance in the Autumn Diesel Gala. Since then, D7017 has been in service for every WSR operating season, completing more than 8,000 miles – with the highest annual mileage (1,440) achieved in 2004 – proving itself to be a consistent and reliable locomotive. Unfortunately, after many years of trouble-free service, during the 2005 Spring Diesel Gala No D7017 failed in service at Blue Anchor with a transmission problem, and was immediately withdrawn from service for repairs, including a full overhaul of the Maybach MD870 engine. It is now back in service as required.

| | |
|---|---|
| Wheel configuration | B-B |
| Wheel diameter | 3ft 9ins |
| Length | 51ft 8½ins |
| Width | 8ft 10ins |
| Height | 12ft 10in |
| Weight | 75t |
| Fuel capacity | 600 gallons |
| Engines | Bristol-Siddeley/Maybach MD870 |
| Transmission | Stone Maybach Mekdro K18U |
| Power output | 1,740bhp @ 1,500rpm |
| Maximum speed | 90mph |
| Tractive effort | Maximum 49,000lbs, continuous 33,950lbs @ 12.5mph |
| Route availability | 7 |
| BR power rating | 3 |

# D7018 'Hymek' Class 35 B-B

No D7018 is seen here in earlier days at Didcot Railway Centre hauling the shuttle service on 5 May 1990. *M. J. Stretton*

## Time Line

**Built:** January 1962
Beyer Peacock

**Known shed allocations:**
1962 Bristol Bath Road
1966 Cardiff Canton
1971 Old Oak Common

**Withdrawn:** July 1975

**Rescued:** 1975

**Arrival at WSR:** July 1990

The second 'Hymek' based on the WSR under the care of the Diesel & Electric Preservation Group – and one of only four members of the class to survive in preservation – is No D7018. Having been completed in January 1962, No D7018's first allocation was to Bristol Bath Road, but this was broken during January and February 1966 with a short spell at Cardiff. In November 1971 a transfer to Old Oak Common took place, from where the locomotive was finally withdrawn on 18 July 1975, four months after No D7017. It was subsequent purchased for preservation by a private individual.

The locomotive was initially stabled at the Great Western Society's base at Didcot, but was later taken over by the Diesel & Electric Preservation Group with a view to it being used as a source of spares for No D7017. However, it was later decided that it should be restored as a working locomotive, and this was undertaken by D&EPG members at Didcot. The weather during the winter of 1979 caused severe frost damage to the engine, which resulted in it receiving a full rebuild. This reached a successful conclusion on 24 August 1985, when the engine was started. No D7018 was initially painted blue with white cab surrounds and small yellow front warning panels, but was subsequently repainted in all-over green livery prior to attending the Old Oak Common Open Day in 1985. As a result of a policy decision by the D&EPG to concentrate all its restoration and maintenance activities at Williton, No D7018 was subsequently moved from Didcot to the WSR in January 1990.

From 1991 the locomotive visited a number of other railways and sites with

No D1010 *Western Campaigner*, including the Great Central and the Mid Hants in early 1994. However, on 19 August 1995, while working the 'Quantock Belle' dining train, No D7018 suffered a major failure, which necessitated its immediate withdrawal from service. Due to pressure from other commitments, work on the repairs did not begin until the autumn of 2002, when the engine was removed and placed on a 'Lowmac' wagon for the bottom end to be stripped down. On 29 March 2004 the locomotive was lifted off its bogies and placed on purpose-built body stands inside the D&EPG's main workshop at Williton. This enabled the bogies, fuel tanks and underframe-mounted equipment to be overhauled more easily. During 2005-06 the bogies were fully overhauled, and the 16 air tanks mounted beneath the underframe removed for inspection. Meanwhile, the Maybach MD870 engine has been completely stripped, and the cause of the failure was discovered to be a cylinder head failure. Currently the engine components are being cleaned, inspected, and made ready for reassembly, while the air tanks were refitted and the bodyshell reunited with the bogies during 2006. It is hoped that No D7018 will be available for service again in 2016, after a successful engine start in late 2015, which will again offer the prospect of seeing two 'Hymek' diesel-hydraulics in service on the WSR.

Technical details for No D7018 are as for D7017 on page 45.

# D9518

## Class 14 0-6-0DH

No D9518, still in the NCB colour scheme, awaits attention and refurbishment. *Keith Smith*

### Time Line

**Built:** October 1964
Swindon Works

**Known shed allocations:**
1964 Cardiff Canton

**Withdrawn:** May 1969

**Rescued:** 1987

**Arrival at WSR:**
4 December 2011

These Type 1 diesel-hydraulics (later Class 14), which eventually totalled 56 locomotives (Nos D9500-55), were all constructed at Swindon Works in 1964-65, the last new class of locomotives to be built there for British Railways. They were primarily designed for working pick-up freight trains and shunting, filling a gap between smaller shunters and main-line diesels. Turned out in two-tone green livery and weighing 51 tons, the class were fitted with a Paxman Ventura 6YJXL engine (650hp) with Voith hydraulic transmission. They had a top speed of approximately 40mph and were fitted with vacuum brakes. However, the design was obsolete even before it left the drawing board, due to the 'Beeching Axe' and the demise of local freight traffic, and all 56 locomotives were withdrawn from service by the early 1970s after a very short time in service.

During their short life on the Western Region, most of the class were used in the Bristol and Cardiff Divisions, but a large number were transferred to Hull (on BR's Eastern Region) a few months before their final withdrawal. Many of the class were subsequently sold out of service to various rail-connected industrial concerns, including the National Coal Board, and British Steel. As a result, no fewer than 19 members of the class have been preserved in the UK

D9518 was completed at Swindon Works in October 1964, and was the 19th member of the class to be built. Its first, and in fact only, allocation was Cardiff Canton, where it remained until withdrawal on 26 1969. In July the locomotive was sold to the National Coal Board and subsequently used at Ashington Colliery in Northumberland, where it became No 7 and was painted into the distinctive Ashington blue livery. Working coal and spoil trains around the network that encompassed Ashington, Ellington, and Lynemouth collieries, occasional trips were made for repairs and routine overhauls to the Lambton Engine works, Philadelphia, these being recorded as taking place in 1975 and 1980. The final overhaul was scheduled for 1986, when the power unit was removed; however, the miners' strike intervened, and the engine was never replaced.

No D9518 was then purchased for preservation, and was moved by road to the Rutland Railway Museum on 26 September 1987, to become a static exhibit. Ownership then passed to the Nene Valley Railway's 'Iron and Steel Traction Group' on 9 September 2006, and the locomotive was retained in NCB blue livery as opposed to the two-tone green livery worn in British Railways service and in which other preserved members of the class were appearing.

As a result of a private purchase by a D&EPG member, the locomotive arrived at Williton on 4 December 2011 to join the existing Class 14, No D9526. Extensive repairs and rebuilding were then carried out to enable the locomotive to enter service again. By the autumn of 2015 No D9518 had been completely stripped to the frames while the major components were receiving attention ready for reinstalling.

Technical details are as No D9526 below.

# D9526 Class 14 0-6-0DH

No D9526 has been fully restored and now looks a real treat in BR two-tone green almost as if the locomotive had just left Swindon Works! *Keith Smith*

## Time Line

**Built:** 1964
Swindon Works

**Known shed allocations:**
1965 Bristol Bath Road
1962 Cardiff Canton

**Withdrawn:** November 1968

**Rescued:** May 1979

**Arrival at WSR:**
3 April 1980

For the history of the Class 14s, see No D9518 above. No D9526 was the second diesel-hydraulic locomotive to arrive on the WSR (the first having been No D7017), and it is again owned by the Diesel & Electric Preservation Group and normally based at its Williton depot.

Built in Swindon in 1964, the locomotive is powered by a Paxman Ventura 6YJXL six-cylinder four-stroke 650hp diesel engine, driving a Voith L217U transmission via a Hunslet triple-reduction and reverse gearbox to a jackshaft. After just five years in British Railways ownership, the locomotive was purchased by Associated Portland Cement (Blue Circle) for use at its works in Westbury, Wiltshire. There it was used for general shunting duties, and is known to have hauled block trains of up to 1,000 tons gross on occasions.

In 1979 the decision was made to dispose of the locomotive, and the Diesel & Electric Group (as it was originally called) set about raising funds to purchase it. The appeal was successful, and No D9526 was moved by road to the WSR, being unloaded at Bishops Lydeard on 3 April 1980. Following movement to the D&EPG's base at Williton two months later, a start was made on overhauling the engine and returning the locomotive to full working order. This reached a successful conclusion on 14 July 1984, when No D9526, fully restored in its former BR two-tone green livery, re-entered service at the WSR's first Diesel Gala event, following a ceremony at Bishops Lydeard.

The locomotive performed regularly on the West Somerset between 1979 and 1993, but was withdrawn again for a full overhaul during the summer of 1993, which was carried out at Williton. By the autumn of 2002 this was more or less complete, except for final painting, and several test runs were carried out. This resulted in No D9526 being returned to service in 2003. The Class 14 has since successfully completed more than 1,500 miles in traffic, much of this hauling the WSR heritage freight train (particularly at special events), although occasional passenger turns have also been recorded.

| | |
|---|---|
| Wheel configuration | 0-6-0 |
| Wheel diameter | 4ft |
| Length over buffers: | 34ft 7in |
| Width | 8ft 7½ins |
| Height | 13ft 0ins |
| Weight | 48t |
| Fuel capacity | 300 gallons |
| Engines | Paxman 6YJXL V6 turbo-charged 26 litres |

| | |
|---|---|
| Transmission | L217 3-speed hydraulic |
| Power output | 650hp @ 1,500rpm |
| Maximum speed | 90mph |
| Tractive effort | Maximum 49,000lbs, continuous 33,950lbs @ 12.5mph |
| BR power rating | 1 |

## Former industrial diesel locomotives

### 24 Ruston & Hornsby 0-4-0DM

Built by the well-known company of Ruston & Hornsby, builder's number 210479, this small four-wheeled diesel locomotive was first delivered to Cadbury's before moving to Bath Gas Works, where it become locomotive No 2. It had a relatively easy working life, being re-engined with an 80hp diesel engine in 1968. Three years later the works stopped producing gas, and the locomotive became redundant. The Somerset & Dorset Railway Circle (as the

No 24 may be one of the smallest locomotives on the WSR but it is one of the busiest stock movers in the preserved railway world! *Keith Smith*

Somerset & Dorset Railway Trust was then known) gave it a home at its Radstock base, where it proved to be of great value moving locomotives and rolling stock around the site. Following the S&DRT's enforced departure from Radstock in the mid-1970s, No 24 was moved, together with the other items of rolling stock in its collection, to the WSR. The small shunter is now based at Washford, where it is used regularly to shunt stock at the S&DRT's base. It has also been claimed that No 24 has the largest buffer beams to be seen anywhere on any engine!

## 1&2 Andrew Barclay 0-4-0DH

These two locomotives were built by Andrew Barclay & Sons at its Kilmarnock Works as recently as 1972, as works numbers 546 and 547, and were supplied new to the Royal Ordnance Factory at Puriton, near Bridgwater. They were capable of working in tandem, and they remained at the factory – which no longer has a connection with the main-line network – until 1991. The pair were then placed on loan with the WSR, arriving during the summer of 1994. Repainted in a dark green livery, Nos 1 and 2 are normally stabled at the Permanent Way depot at Dunster, from where they are used on engineering trains.

*Above and left:* Nos 1 and 2 are based at Dunster and haul engineering trains,; the best chance of seeing them in action is probably when the railway is closed to normal traffic. *Keith Smith*

# Diesel multiple units

Diesel multiple units (DMUs) – or diesel railcars as they are sometimes referred to – have been a common sight on the West Somerset Railway since the line was reopened in 1976. Although their use has declined in recent years, they remain an important part of train operation on the WSR, being used mainly to support the railway's steam fleet at busier periods and during times of heavy traffic, and also for charter work.

## DMU Class 115 Derby Suburban 3 or 4-car unit

These DMUs were built in 1962 by British Railways at Derby for use either as a three-car sets (DMBS-TCL-DMBS) or four-car sets (DMBS-TS-TCL-DMBS). The former were gangway-fitted, and were allocated to Allerton, while the latter sets were allocated to London Marylebone for use on the Chiltern line. Five Class 115 power cars (DMBS) and one trailer car (TCL) are preserved on the WSR. Nos 51887, 51663, 51880 and 51859 are also DMBS types, all being purchased by the WSR after having been displaced by the new 'Turbo' units in the Chilterns. Gangways have been fitted to the cars not previously provided with them, and as an extra feature the interior door between the guard's compartment and the saloon has been enlarged to enable easy access for wheelchair passengers, resulting in a small loss in seating capacity. It is interesting to note that Nos 51663 and 51887 were fitted with power sanding equipment during the mid-1980s using equipment recovered from withdrawn Class 25 diesel locomotives. The units are regularly employed on passenger services. Each DMBS was fitted with a Leyland Albion 200hp diesel engine, and seated 78

'Not in Service' reads the destination box as the Class 115 makes progress towards Blue Anchor. *Steve Edge*

2nd Class passengers before modification. They weigh 38½ tons, and are 19.5 metres long by 2.82 metres wide. Due to the poor condition of its bodywork, No 51663 has subsequently been withdrawn from service, with the frames expected to become a mobile advertisement hoarding for the railway, positioned near to the main-line network at Norton Fitzwarren. At the end of January 2007 No 51889 emerged from the Minehead workshops after a major rebuild and repaint into the original dark green livery with yellow end panel. No 51859 then took its place for similar treatment. They are both to be reinstated in traffic following the return of the green DMU that was owned by the Army, which left in January 2007 for an MoD establishment.

DMU

## Class 117 Pressed Steel Suburban 3-Car Unit

Built by Pressed Steel in 1959-60, these vehicles were originally non-gangwayed, but on arrival at the WSR they were gangway-fitted. Our examples are Nos 59493, 59505 and 59515, which are all TCLs (Trailer Composite Lavatory). No 59514 is now no longer used in traffic as a result of fire damage, but the remaining vehicles are painted in dark green, and are used to supplement the locomotive-hauled sets at peak periods and Galas. Each seats 22 1st Class and 48 2nd Class passengers in two open saloons separated by two toilets and a centre corridor. Their weight is 30½ tons, and they are 19.46 metres long by 2.82 metres wide.

The Class 117 unit approaches Blue Anchor. *Keith Smith*

# Passenger rolling stock

## Former BR passenger stock

From the early 1950s onwards, British Railways began constructing passenger coaches to new standard designs. They incorporated the better features of many of the older designs, and were intended to be lighter on maintenance. All the coaching stock used in regular passenger service on the West Somerset Railway is from the original Mark 1 series, many of which have undergone extensive refurbishment over recent years to prolong their active life. These vehicles are fitted with vacuum brakes and steam heating, although some also have air brakes fitted.

## Mark 1 First Open (FO)

**No 3018**
Originally built at Swindon in 1962 under Lot 30697, this coach later passed into the ownership of Flying Scotsman Services, which used it as part of its maroon-liveried charter set; it was subsequently TOPS-plated with the number 99358. After a period of service on hire to the Bluebell Railway, it became one of four FOs put up for sale while stabled at Ferne Park sidings, Bounds Green, London, in October 1991. Purchased by the WSRA, No 3108 was delivered by road to Bishops Lydeard the following month, and is now part of the Association's 'Quantock Belle' dining train. Seating 42 in a 2+1 arrangement, the coach carries 'Quantock Belle' livery, and the name *Meteor*.

**No 3058**
Originally built in Doncaster in 1955 to Lot 30169 as the first of its batch, this is a standard Mark 1 design weighing 33 tons and seating 42 1st Class passengers. After 17 years in passenger service, it was condemned at Newcastle Central, but was converted for TOPS use and given the departmental number TDB975313. Acquired from Exeter by the 5542 Group during 1983, the coach was purchased by WSR plc in 1989 for conversion into another service train buffet. No 3058 entered passenger service on the WSR during Easter 1990.

**No 3131**
Built Swindon in 1963 to Lot No 30717 and Diagram 73, this coach is dual-braked and seats 42 passengers on a 2+1 basis. Purchased by the WSRA from Riviera Trains as an additional seating vehicle for the 'Quantock Belle' set, it arrived at Williton on 4 April 2013, and is in maroon livery.

## Mark I Second Open (SO)

**No 4814**
Built in 1959 as part of Lot 30473 by the Birmingham Railway Carriage & Wagon Company for the London Midland Region of British Railways, this vehicle was transferred to the Eastern Region during 1965. It was condemned in York in 1976. Open Seconds had the greatest variation of any BR Mark 1 design and appeared in a good many train formations. An additional benefit was that they could be marshalled next to a kitchen car to provide extra restaurant seating. The coach originally seated 64 2nd Class passengers on a 2+1 basis in eight bays. No 4814 was one of the first passenger coaches to arrive on the WSR. During the winter of 1980-81 it was rebuilt as a First Open using seats recovered from 2nd Class Pullman coaches. A small micro-buffet was installed at one end, and the exterior was given an all-red livery. For use during the GWR 150 celebrations in 1985, the coach was refitted inside with a buffet/bar and loose seating. Further work was carried out in 1987 to repanel the interior walls and refit the bar, with an exterior repaint in chocolate and cream. No 4814 received a complete refurbishment in the first half of 1992, and is now a regular sight as a general catering vehicle on service trains.

## Mark I Tourist Second Open (TSO)

All the TSOs seat 64 passengers in a 2+1 arrangement, are steam heated and vacuum braked, and have a tare weight of 33 tons.

**No 4260**
This former Eastern Region coach was built by the Birmingham Railway Carriage & Wagon Company in 1956 under Lot 30207 to Diagram 93. Condemned at Bristol in January 1983, it was purchased privately and moved to the WSR in May 1983. Now in regular service train use, the vehicle ran more than 40,000 miles in traffic between 1992 and 1994.

**No 4346**
Built in 1956 for British Railways under Lot 30207 to Diagram 93, again by the Birmingham Railway Carriage & Wagon Company, this coach was condemned in March 1976. After use as a staff accommodation coach on the WSR, it is now being extensively rebuilt and converted into a further bar and buffet car for future use on service trains. During the autumn of 2015 it became the second in the service fleet, after No 5030, to receive the new 'blood and custard' livery.

**No 4419**
Built by the Birmingham Railway Carriage & Wagon Company under Lot 30226 to Diagram 93 in 1956, this vehicle was purchased from Carlisle having seen use on the West Highland line in Scotland. Now a regular member of the WSR service train fleet, the coach recorded 43,000 miles in traffic between 1992 and 1994.

## Mark I Tourist Second Open (TSO) *continued*

**No 4435**

Building details are the same as No 4419 above. The coach was purchased from Bounds Green depot, London, by the Home Counties Group of the WSRA. The funds were raised as a result of the Group's sales stand activities at various events throughout the country, and from the profits made from sales of previous editions of the WSR Stock Book. When it arrived on the railway in 1990, the livery carried was green and cream, reflecting its use on the Fort William to Mallaig steam specials, that livery having been introduced originally by the LNER for its tourist trains. The vehicle has since been repainted in chocolate and cream.

No 4435 was the first coach to receive a major overhaul in the carriage works at Minehead, including the replacement of the ends and removal of one toilet to provide a larger end vestibule. This time it was outshopped in the BR(WR) style of chocolate and cream, and a small brass plaque is fixed to the interior vestibule wall to mark its return to service on the WSR.

**No 4449**

Again built by the Birmingham Railway Carriage & Wagon Company in 1956 under Lot 30226 to Diagram 93, this coach was latterly sent to Moreton-on-Lugg, Herefordshire, as an instruction coach, and given the number TDM977413. It was purchased by the WSR from there, arriving in June 1988.

**No 4599**

This example was built under Lot 30243 to Diagram 93 at York in 1958. On arrival on the WSR it was originally allocated to the 'Quantock Belle' set but, following refurbishment, it is now in general service train use resplendent in chocolate and cream.

**No 4660**

Also built at York, but under Lot 30375 to Diagram 93 in 1957, and purchased from Thornton Fields, London, this vehicle was completely refurbished at Minehead during 1992-93, and is now part of the regular service train fleet.

**No 4875**

Built under Lot 30525 to Diagram 89 at Wolverton in 1959, this coach has a tare weight of 35 tons and is carried on B4 bogies. Purchased from HSBC, it arrived on the line early in 2002, carrying Regional Railways blue livery, having been used on the North Wales coast line.

**No 4876**

Details as the same as No 4875 above, but this coach is now painted in WSR chocolate and cream livery, and entered service during the 2006 Spring Steam Gala.

**No 4884**

Also built under Lot 30525 to Diagram 89 at Wolverton in 1959, No 4884 arrived on the WSR in the autumn of 1994.

**No 4909**

Built under Lot 30646 to Diagram 89 at Wolverton in 1961, this coach arriving on the WSR in August 2000 after purchase from Rail Charter Services at Bounds Green.

Mark I TSO No 5030. *Keith Smith*

**No 4911**
Built at BR's Wolverton Works in 1960, also under Lot 30646 to Diagram 89, like No 4419 this coach was purchased from Carlisle, where it had been stored after seeing use on the West Highland line. It arrived on the West Somerset in early 1991, and ran for several years in green and cream livery. No 4911 received an extensive overhaul in the Minehead Carriage Works in early 1995 and is used regularly on service trains.

**No 4956**
Technical details are as for No 4987 below; however, No 4956 was used on charter services until placed on the tender list by what was then EWS in April 2009. Successfully purchased by the WSRA's Home Counties Group and joining Nos 4435 and 5024 in the Group's fleet, No 4956 arrived at Bishops Lydeard by road in May 2009, and entered service after minor work, including a complete re-upholster. Bearing the BR blue and grey livery, it has since been repainted into standard WSR chocolate and cream.

**No 4987**
Originally built at Wolverton in 1961 under Lot 30690 to Diagram 89, this coach was converted to a training coach and located at the former Bristol Bath Road depot, and given the departmental number ADB977706.

**No 5002**
Also built at Wolverton in 1962, this example was purchased from EWS at Old Oak Common depot in January 2006. Having been repainted from BR blue and grey to chocolate and cream, the coach entered passenger service on the WSR in the summer of 2006.

## Mark I Tourist Second Open (TSO) *continued*

**No 5024**
Again built at Wolverton in 1962 under Lot 30690 to Diagram 89, this coach was refurbished by British Rail in the 1980s with bright laminate interior panels, striped upholstery and strip lighting. Latterly painted in Network SouthEast livery, it saw out its days on the London Paddington to Oxford/Newbury services before the introduction of the 'Thames Turbos'. Withdrawn at Old Oak Common, it was purchased by the WSRA Home Counties Group, becoming the second Mark I owned by the Group. Fitted at the time of purchase with B4 bogies, which BR wished to retain, the coach made a round trip to Cardiff Cathays for B1 bogies to be fitted in their place. Delivered to Bishops Lydeard by road on 15 March 1993, the vehicle was put into immediate service by painting over the blue lower body panel with brown. No 5024 has since received a full repaint into WSR colours, and in May 2000 the B1 bogies were replaced with a set of redundant B4 bogies. A regular coach on timetabled services, it re-entered service in 2006 after overhaul.

**No 5025**
Building details are as No 5024 above. It arrived on the WSR in 2002 following purchase from Riviera Trains, and already carried BR(WR) chocolate and cream livery.

**No 5030**
Details are as No 5024/25 above. However, in 2015, due to a change of policy whereby the dual-braked coaches were to be identified differently, this vehicle was the first to appear in the new red and cream ('blood and custard') livery.

## Mark I Corridor Second (SK)

All the SKs seat 64 passengers in eight compartments with access to these and the toilets at each end being by a side corridor. The vehicles are 64ft 6in long, with a tare weight of 32 tons, and were built to Diagram 146.

**No 24985**
Built by British Railways at Derby in 1956 to Lot 30208, this coach was initially sold to the Dart Valley Railway, which used it on its Paignton to Kingswear branch. It was one of a batch of four SKs purchased from the DVLR by WSR plc in 1989 to strengthen the railway's passenger fleet.

**No 25308**
Built at Wolverton to Lot 30349 in 1957, this was another of the vehicles purchased from the DVLR in 1989. It entered passenger service soon after its arrival, even though it carried DVR livery, which is very similar to that of the WSR. It was renumbered 18308 by BR but, following a complete refurbishment and exterior repaint at Minehead in 1993, reverted to its original running number.

Mark I SK No 24985. *Keith Smith*

**No 25323**
Building details are as for No 25308. This ex-DVR coach also arrived in 1989.

**No 25454**
Built at Wolverton to Lot 30350 in 1957, this was the fourth of the vehicles purchased from the DVLR in 1989.

## Mark I Brake Corridor Second (BSK)

When built, the BSKs were vacuum-braked, steam-heated, and weighed 35 tons. Half the coach consisted of a guard's compartment and luggage area, while the other half consisted of four 2nd Class compartments seating 24 passengers, accessed by a side corridor. All were built to Diagram 181.

**No 35257**
Built by British Railways at its Wolverton Works in 1958 under Lot 30427, the WSRA Stock Fund purchased this vehicle from Nunnery Sidings, Sheffield. From there it was moved by rail to Bridgwater, then on to the WSR by road, arriving in June 1981. The coach was extensively refurbished in Minehead Carriage Works during the first half of 1993, and half of the former luggage area was converted and fitted out for the use of passengers in wheelchairs. No 35257 is a regular member of the WSR service fleet.

**No 35408**
Built at Wolverton to Diagram 181 under Lot 30721, this vehicle passed to Balfour Beatty for engineering use as

## Mark 1 Brake Corridor Second (BSK) *continued*

A Mark 1 Brake Corridor Second (BSK). *Keth Smith*

part of 'Project Mercury'. Extensive modification took place, such as the removal of the corridor connections and provision of a small electrical generator. Purchased by the WSRA for use in the 'Quantock Belle' set, it is being further modified to include a pantry, and the generator is being retained to allow train heating without the use of an attached steam locomotive, as well as to power freezers, etc. Painted in 'Quantock Belle' colours, it is now named *Juniper*.

## Mark 1 Brake Second Open (BSO)

When built, the BSOs originally had seating for 39 passengers, arranged in five bays, and were fitted with vacuum brakes and steam heating. The vehicles are 64ft 6in long and weigh 33 tons. A number of internal modifications were carried out to the vehicles when in service with BR and subsequently. The BSO design is ideally suited for use on the WSR.

**No 9227**

This is the oldest of the three BSO vehicles now based on the WSR, but the most recent arrival. Built by British Railways at Doncaster Works in 1956 to Lot 30170, Diagram 183, it spent a lot of time working on the Eastern Region, later carrying the number E3227. Purchased by the Scottish Railway Preservation Society in 1988 for use in its main-line-registered rake of stock, it was renumbered SCR99821 and repainted in BR lined maroon. The vehicle is dual-braked and dual-heated, and arrived on the WSR in May 2006.

**No 9278**

Also built at Doncaster in 1956, but under Lot 30244, Diagram 183, for the Eastern Region, this coach was initially only employed on excursion trains, but latterly saw more general use on BR. It was one of the earliest arrivals on the West Somerset Railway and has run regularly on the line since. Seating is arranged in five bays accommodating 39 2nd Class passengers, and is equipped with BR1 bogies, vacuum brakes, and steam heating.

**No 9380**

Built in 1963 to Lot 30698 at Wolverton, this vehicle was converted to a BSO(T) in 1980 by removing one seating bay and replacing it with counter space and a catering trolley. The adjacent toilet was removed and converted into a steward's washing area and store, seating being reduced to 31 2nd Class passengers. On withdrawal from BR service, it was purchased for use on the Llangollen Railway, where it entered service as the brake vehicle on the 'Berwyn Belle' dining train. After it was decided to withdraw the dining train from service, No 9380 was put up for sale and purchased by WSR plc in March 2002. It entered public service during the 2002 Spring Steam Gala, initially in maroon livery, but has subsequently been repainted in chocolate and cream.

## Mark I Corridor Brake First (BFK)

**No W17015**

Built at Swindon in 1959 to Diagram 161, under Lot 30668, this coach weighs 36 tons and seats 24 1st Class passengers. It is not part of the service fleet, but is the main-line support coach to *Kinlet Hall.* Easily identified by its red and cream livery, it has been given the TOPS number 99792.

## Mark I Brake Corridor Composite (BCK)

When built, the BCKs had two 1st Class and three 2nd Class compartments in one half, and a guard's compartment and luggage area in the other. Seating was for 12 1st Class passengers and either 18 or 24 2nd Class, depending on whether the compartment seats had arm rests fitted. The vehicle's tare weight is 35 tons, and they were built to Diagram 171.

**No 21174**

Built in 1958 by Charles Roberts to Lot 30424, the coach was originally purchased in 1982, while lying at Castle Cary, by a group of WSR volunteers for use as the brake vehicle in the 'Quantock Belle' dining train. Following repainting into maroon, and bearing the name *Phoenix*, the coach entered WSR service on 6 August 1983. It is now owned by the WSRA.

## Mark I Miniature Buffet (RMB)

**No 1804**
This coach was built at York under Lot 30485 to Diagram 97 during 1957, and is basically a Mark I Second Open (SO) with two full window spaces removed to accommodate a buffet counter, and a further four seats removed to allow provision of a stock cupboard. Steam heating and vacuum braking were provided as standard. This vehicle, which was originally numbered SC1804, ran on the Scottish Region of BR, and was purchased privately from Perth at the end of 1981. It was delivered by rail to Bridgwater, then by road to Bishops Lydeard, arriving in late January 1982. For the 1986 season No 1804 was painted in a modified 'Pullman' livery, and given the name *Aries*, forming part of the 'Quantock Belle' dining train. During 1993 the stock cupboard was converted to form a washing-up space within the buffet area, and the exterior was repainted in maroon. In addition to its dining train duties, the coach sees occasional use on WSR service trains during peak periods and at special events. It is now owned by the WSRA and is in Quantock Belle livery.

## Mark I Unclassified Restaurant (RUB)

**No 1909**
Originally numbered W1909, this coach is a catering vehicle built under Lot 30401 to Diagram 23 in 1957 as an 'Unclassified Restaurant' (RU). A later modification with a transverse counter allowed it to be reclassified as an RU(B). Seating is for 29 in loose chairs. It has a tare weight of 39 tons, and the customary steam heating and vacuum braking are fitted. Allocated to the Western Region, the coach was withdrawn from service at Old Oak Common, from where a WSRA member purchased it privately with assistance from the WSRA Home Counties Group. The coach's last BR journey was to Bridgwater, from where it moved by road to Bishops Lydeard, arriving in June 1981. Also allocated to the 'Quantock Belle' dining train, it was repainted in the same livery as No 1804 at the start of 1986, and carries the name *Orion*. During 1993 the coach was repainted into lined maroon livery, the same as the other three vehicles in the 'QB' rake. It received a major overhaul and refit at Minehead Carriage Works during 1995-96, and is also now in the Quantock Belle livery

## District Engineer's Saloon

**No W80976 (TDW80976)**
At the end of the Second World War the District Engineer's Saloons of the Great Western were in need of replacement. To a design by Hawksworth, six were built at Swindon under Lot 1701 to Diagram Q13 in 1948. They were 52 feet long and 8ft 11in wide, and were carried on pressed steel bogies with a 9-foot wheelbase.

The design consisted of an open saloon at each end split by a guard's area, toilet and small kitchen compartment. Large windows were a feature of the ends, as were retractable steps on each side in the middle of the vehicle. Our example became the Taunton Area District Engineer's Saloon, but was sold into preservation, entering a private site at the preserved Rowden Mill station on the old Leominster to Worcester line. Considerable work was carried out on the coach, but it was put up for sale and purchased by the WSRA. Arriving on the West Somerset Railway in mid-July 2012, its inaugural run was on 8 December 2013 with the 'Quantock Belle'. No W80976 is now available for private hire, and further details are available from the West Somerset Railway Association on 01823 433856, or by email at info@wsra.org.uk.

No W80976, the District Engineer's Saloon. *Keith Smith*

## Mark I Gangwayed Brake (BG)

All Mark I BGs are on the shorter 57-foot frames, and have a load capacity of 10 tons. BR1 bogies were originally fitted, the maximum permitted speed being 90mph. They were built to Diagram 711.

**No 80736**

Built in 1955 as part of Lot 30140 by the Birmingham Railway Carriage & Wagon Company, this coach was originally classified 'NDV'. It was purchased by the WSRA in 1990, donated to WSR plc, and converted in the Minehead Carriage Works to a vehicle specially designed for the conveyance of wheelchair and other passengers. This work involved the removing of four pairs of double doors, and fitting a new frame and skin. One end as been fitted out as a saloon with six pairs of standard Mark I windows, while at the other end a large toilet compartment has been installed. To allow easy access for wheelchairs, the gangway passing the guard's compartment was widened, which involved moving the emergency toolbox. Good-quality floor material was fitted throughout, and special rails affixed to the floor, to which 10 or 12 wheelchairs can be safely secured. Some fixed seating was also installed. Access to the coach is via two wide doors, each fitted with a hydraulic lift, which can raise or lower a wheelchair occupant from or to rail level if necessary. One of the lifts was generously donated to the project

## Mark I Gangwayed Brake (BG) *continued*

by its manufacturer, Ratcliff Tail-lifts. Externally, the coach was painted in WSR colours and christened *Lorna Doone*. No 80736 sees regular use on the WSR, running more than 45,000 miles between 1992 and 1994 alone. It is also available for hire.

Mark I Gangwayed Brake No 80736 at Minehead. *Keith Smith*

**No 80742**
Built in 1959 as part of Lot 30140 by the Birmingham Railway Carriage & Wagon Company as No 80736 above, it was also classified 'NDV'. After purchase from Reading in 1990 the coach was painted in maroon livery and served as the brake coach in the 'Quantock Belle' set. The vehicle is currently stored out of use at Minehead.

Mark I Gangwayed Brake No 80972. *Keith Smith*

**No 80972**
Built in York in 1956 under Lot 30173, this vehicle was purchased by WSR plc in 1990. Now painted grey, it has been fitted out as a mobile stores and workshop for the Signal & Telegraph Department. It played a valuable support role in the Crowcombe Heathfield resignalling project, completed in May 1994.

## Ex-BR No M31407M

**NoxXDB977037**
Although built by British Railways, this vehicle is actually of London Midland & Scottish Railway (LMS) origin. It dates back to 1950, having been constructed at Derby under Lot 1579 to Diagram 2171, and allocated the running number M31407M. A post-war 50-foot gangwayed brake (BG) of 12-tons capacity, the Diagram was very similar to the LMS Diagrams D1854 and D2007 for a 'Period III' coach, except that no raised beading was fitted at the waist and above the windows. Converted in

1981 to a stores van – this was probably when the gangways were removed – and renumbered XBD977037, it was allocated to Crewe Stationary Stores. Having been in store at Thingley Junction, Chippenham, it arrived on the West Somerset Railway in 1996 at the same time as SR Bulleid 'Pacific' No 34053 *Sir Keith Park* (which has since departed from the line). Now privately owned and based at Williton, after some time in use as a stores van a start has been made on restoring it to original condition.

## High Security Brake Van (NBA)

**No 94442**
Classified 'NBA', this vehicle's full title is 'High Security Brake Van', and it was modified with sealed gangways, new floors, built-in tail lights, and roller shutter doors. Riding on B4 bogies and rated at 100mph, it weighs 31.4 tons. Previous running numbers were 80932 and 92723. No 94442 arrived on the WSR with No 94148.

## Former GWR passenger stock

A number of interesting and historic former Great Western Railway coaches are based on the West Somerset Railway, though none are in regular passenger service on the line.

## Corridor Third

**No 2573**
Built as a 57-foot Corridor Third by the Great Western Railway, and known as a 'Multibar Toplight', this vehicle was completed under Lot 1234 during February 1914, the Diagram number being C32. British Railways condemned the coach during 1957, and in December of that year it was converted into a camping coach at Swindon. It appeared in all-over green livery and was sent to Dawlish Warren; after only a year it was repainted chocolate and cream. Renumbered to 9879, and later to just 79, the coach was named *Carol* during the 1960s, when all camping coaches were allocated a five-character female name. It was finally withdrawn from service at the end of the 1980 season and taken by rail to Exeter, while some withdrawn catering vehicles were converted to become replacements at Dawlish. No 9879 was privately purchased and sent by road to the WSR, first to Bishops Lydeard, then to the disused down platform line at Crowcombe. During 1982 the old camping coach siding at Blue Anchor was reinstated, and No 9879 is now one of three such vehicles that resides there.

**No 2578**
The building details for this coach are as for No 2573 above. Having been condemned by BR in 1956, it was also converted into a camping coach

## Corridor Third *continued*

and sent to Marazion near Penzance, being allocated the number 9889. In 1962 it was moved to St Agnes and the following year joined Nos 9887 and 9888 at Blue Anchor. When BR ceased operations on the branch at the start of 1971, No 9889 was privately purchased and moved to Minehead via Taunton. The coach was transferred into the care of the Somerset & Dorset Railway Trust, and was stabled at Washford for use by volunteers. In late 1994 it was resold to the WSRA, and moved by rail to Williton, where it stood on a short plinth of track adjacent to the former Swindon shed and was used by the Association's steam locomotive restoration team. In June 2006 No 2578 was craned back onto the main running line and is a long-term project for restoration.

### No 3639

This coach was built by the GWR at Swindon in 1910 to Diagram C31. In 1915 it was converted into a Royal Ambulance coach and was probably sent to France for war service. After the war it was reconverted to a Corridor Third with eight compartments, and worked throughout the Great Western system. Again it is believed to have seen war service during the Second World War when, in 1940, it was possibly sent to Dover for Dunkirk evacuation train duties. No 3639 was condemned in 1956, when it was converted into a camping coach and renumbered 9887. From 1957 it resided in a siding at Blue Anchor until the closure of the Minehead branch in early 1971, whereupon it was purchased by a WSRA member.

### No 3668

Like No 3639, this coach was also built by the GWR at Swindon in 1910, and saw war service on ambulance train duties in France, being repatriated in 1918. Originally a 57-foot 'Toplight' of the 'Bars I' design, it was reconverted in 1922 under Lot 1313 to Diagram C35 as an eight-compartment Corridor Third. No 3668 was withdrawn in 1956 to become camping coach No 9888 based at Blue Anchor until 1971. It was then purchased by a WSRA member and stabled on a short length of track at Crowcombe beside the former quarry siding. By the latter part of the 1990s volunteer accommodation on the West Somerset was starting to become a problem, especially at the Bishops Lydeard end of the line, and No 3668 was chosen as a solution. Conversion started in 1997, after the vehicle was moved from Crowcombe, to provide accommodation for eight; this comprised a kitchen, lounge, three bedrooms, and toilet, complete with electric heating and lighting, smoke alarms, and fire protection. It is now set on a small length of track within the Locomotive Compound at Bishops Lydeard.

### No 3885

This coach is another ex-Dawlish Warren example and is also the youngest, having been completed in July 1920. Again, a 57-foot Corridor Third of the 'Multibar Toplight' variety, it was built under Lot No 1269 and Diagram C32. With the building of the new British Railways Mark I stock, the coach was renumbered 3385 during 1955. Its later history is very similar to that of No 2573 above, except that it was christened *Hilda* and renumbered 9882, then just 82. The coach is also located at Blue Anchor, and is owned by the Home Counties Group of the West Somerset Railway Association, which uses it as a base for working volunteers on the railway.

'Toplight' No 3885 located at Blue Anchor. *Keith Smith*

**No 3980**
Constructed to Diagram C35 during November 1917 under Lot 1256 as a 57-foot 'Toplight' Corridor Third of the 'Bars 1' variety, the vehicle's history parallels that of No 9879, being converted to a camping coach in December 1957, given the name *Elsie* and sent to Dawlish Warren. It was later renumbered 9881, then 81. Purchased by a WSRA member, it arrived on the WSR in the same manner as No 9879. It is based at Blue Anchor.

## Brake Corridor Composite

**No 6705**
Built at Swindon in 1938 to a design by Collett under Lot 1589, Diagram E159, it was withdrawn from traffic in 1967, overhauled at Swindon, and shipped to a railway museum in Vermont, USA. It was later transferred to Scranton, Pennsylvania, then donated to the West Somerset Railway Steam Trust. It was shipped back to the UK from Halifax, Nova Scotia, on board the MV *Fairlift*, together with a consignment of new Class 66 diesel locomotives. Arriving at Newport on 26 February 2007, it was taken to Crewe for restoration work. No 6705 was complete inside, but the buffers and couplings used on British railways had been replaced by 'buck-eye' couplings. Arriving at Williton in early 2012 for finishing work, the coach is now available for carrying passengers although, because of its historical nature, it will only be used on special occasions.

The much-travelled No 6705 *Keith Smith*

# Corridor Composite

**No 7740**

The Great Western Railway built 18 Corridor Composites at Swindon in 1911 to Diagram E88 under Lot 1711. The sole survivor is No 7740, which, after more than 40 years in passenger service with the GWR and BR, was converted into a Mess & Tool Van in June 1955, and renumbered DW317. After use by the Signal & Telegraph Department at West Ealing, it stood for some time at Old Oak Common surplus to requirements. An Association member purchased the coach, and it arrived on the WSR in March 1977, being used initially as an accommodation coach for volunteers.

Corridor Composite No 7740. *Chris Austin*

More recently, No 7740 has been based at Minehead and used as a staff training room, but is now in store awaiting a decision on its future.

# Bogie Gangwayed Milk Van ('Siphon G')

**No W2980**

The Bogie Gangwayed Milk Van – or 'Siphon G' to give it its GWR telegraphic code name – was designed specifically to carry milk churns. Built with a wooden ventilated body on a metal underframe, the floors were of concrete to facilitate the cooling of churns in transit. No W2980 was built at Swindon during 1930 to Diagram O33, and classified as a 'brown vehicle', being registered on the passenger vehicle list. Being 50 feet long, vacuum-braked, and fitted with steam-heating through pipes, these vehicles could be marshalled at either end of a passenger train should the need arise.

'Siphon G' No W2980 awaiting restoration. *Keith Smith*

Two WSRA members originally purchased this example from Swindon in May 1979, but it is now owned by the 813 Fund. While under restoration in 2002, a coat of military green paint was discovered under the existing paint, and further investigation suggested that the vehicle had formed part of a Second World War ambulance train, possibly one working from Netley Marsh Hospital, near Southampton. Restoration was completed at Williton in September 2002, and the vehicle now carries the original brown GWR livery.

**No W1046**

This particular 'Siphon G' was actually built by British Railways at Swindon to Diagram O62, Lot 1768, in 1955 to a Great Western design. Due to the decline in milk storage in churns, the vehicle was fitted out as a newspaper van in the 1970s, the bodywork vents being sealed up, benches fitted, and strip lighting installed. In this role newspapers could be sorted and bound up for delivery to the various wholesalers en route ready for onward delivery to newsagents. No 1046 is privately owned and currently awaits restoration.

## Auto-trailer

The popular auto-trailer No W169 awaits departure from Minehead during the Spring 2008 Gala. The visiting 0-4-2T No 1450 is sandwiched between No W169 and visiting No W158. *Peter Townsend*

**No W169**

For some time the GWR used 'railmotors' on branch-line duties, which consisted of a single car capable of being driven from both ends, and fitted with a small vertical boiler driving a power bogie. They were later converted to trailers, with the engine removed, and coupled to a tank locomotive specially fitted with auto-gear to enable the train to be driven from the coach end as well as from the footplate. This avoided the need for the engine to have to run round its train at each end of each journey. Ultimately, new auto-trailers were built, and in 1929 another batch of 12 was constructed under Lot 1394. Built to a new design with flush sides, they had one large smoking compartment, and a small non-smoking saloon at the rear, separated by a guard's compartment. Also of note were eight tip-up seats in the luggage area to cater for overcrowding. The saloon seats were heavy mahogany, with mahogany window frames and panelling above the seats. Externally, the bow-ended coaches were 59ft 6in long and 9 feet wide, riding on 7-foot-pattern bogies.

The non-driving end windows were painted out in black in February 1935, and totally panelled over after 1948. Various liveries were carried throughout their lives, from the standard Great Western chocolate and cream, all-over brown, and all maroon. It is known that the cream, brown and gold livery was applied in September 1931, and an all-brown livery with orange strip appeared in 1943, at least for the duration of the war. An unusual feature was the external steps, which extended outwards for use at halts at ground level, being controlled by a lever in the centre vestibule. Seating was for a total of 72.

No W169 was recorded as having worked from Merthyr, Aberdare, Cardiff, Nelson, Caerphilly and Gloucester, before being condemned in November 1961. However, a month later it was reinstated as an internal vehicle and given the number 064749, being allocated to the Locomotive Department at Gloucester. Condemned again in 1982, it entered preservation, initially on the Gloucestershire Warwickshire Railway, before ending up at Wallingford. After the success of using sister coach No W178, and the fitting of West Somerset locomotives Nos 6412 and 5542 with auto-trailer control gear, a search was made to see if an auto-trailer of our own could be acquired. This led to the purchase of No W169 by the 5542 Locomotive Group from the Cholsey & Wallingford Railway, and it arrived on the WSR on 9 November 2004. A positive start has been made on the restoration of the vehicle at Williton.

## Sleeping Car

### No 9038

Historically speaking, the most valuable item of rolling stock currently based on the WSR is No 9038. The Great Western Railway built three sleeping cars at Swindon in February 1897 to Diagram J5, under Lot 787, for use on the London Paddington to Milford Haven and Plymouth boat trains. Normally used singly, with one held spare, they consisted of eight 1st Class berths with a central compartment used either as a day saloon, or by the attendant. Each pair of sleeping compartments shared a toilet, accessible from either, but a clever lever arrangement prevented the occupant of one compartment entering the toilet when in use by the other sharer. Included in each compartment was a small folding wash basin and small folding

GWR Sleeping Car No 9038. *Keith Smith*

table, and in our example these items can still be seen, even though most interior walls had been removed. When in use, the attendant would lock the end doors to the corridor connection, allowing access to the coach only by the two central doors, which were under supervision. A small end compartment contained a stove and sink, from where the attendant was able to supply light refreshments, while a separate toilet was situated at the other end. Generally, the internal finishings were mahogany, with sycamore panels. Some scenic photographs remain, dating from the early 1920s. Externally, the body is 56 feet long by 9 feet wide, and carried on 10-foot bogies.

During 1931 all three vehicles were withdrawn, with No 9038 being sold off in 1933 as living accommodation at Burton, near Stogursey in Somerset. After delivery it was incorporated into a bungalow, where it remained until 1986, when the premises were rebuilt, and the body was donated to the railway. After resting in a nearby field, it was delivered to the WSR on 24 September 1986 and placed on the underframe of ex-GWR Collett BCK No 6912, which had been acquired from the Severn Valley Railway. As the underframe was slightly too long, the body was lifted off again, a small section removed from the centre of the frames, the two ends welded back together again, and the body refitted.

After a comprehensive and painstaking restoration, carried out by the West Somerset Steam Railway Trust at Williton, No 9038 ran in service for the first time on 13 May 2006, with a series of special runs for invited guests after a ceremonial recommissioning by Lady Elizabeth Gass, Lord Lieutenant of Somerset.

## Former Somerset & Dorset Joint Railway passenger stock

### 1st Class Coach No 4

Built at Highbridge in 1886, this coach was possibly the first to wear the now famous Prussian Blue livery, and it was also one of the first six-wheeled coaches to be built for the line. It seems that it was converted for internal use in 1911 and lasted in engineering service until the body was sold around 1930 to Templecombe Parish Council, which used it as a sports pavilion in Templecombe until 1986, when it was presented to the Somerset & Dorset Railway Trust. Work on restoration started in 1988. The body was originally placed on an LNWR 'CCT' chassis, but is now on a more correct style of LMS chassis. Full restoration was almost complete by the start of 2016, when it is hoped that it will carry its first passengers at Galas and other special occasions.

S&DJR 1st Class Coach No 4. *Keith Smith*

# Freight stock

A very interesting and varied collection of goods wagons is based on the West Somerset Railway. Some are used regularly on civil engineering trains, while others have historic interest and form part of the railway's demonstration heritage goods train, which is often seen running at Gala events and other special occasions.

It should be noted that while every effort is made by both the owners of freight stock and the railway to obtain authenticity wherever possible, the original numbers and identity of some items may have been lost in the various changes of ownership over the years. Therefore some numbers carried may only be representative of the type of wagon, and not the true original number.

## Box vans

### MoD No 47983

Built for the Ministry of Defence in 1940 by the Southern Railway, and registered by that company in 1943 as No 1132, this van was marshalled in Workshop Train No 10 as the generator van, to see service in France. Painted plain green, there are unusual holes in the end where the exhaust and cables entered, and an entrance door and small platform can be seen over one of the buffers. There is also shelving fitted inside. Privately owned and in general use, the wagon was repaired and given a repaint into full MoD livery in time for the 2004 Spring Steam Gala.

MoD box van No 47983. *Keith Smith*

### RNAD No 229

Obtained from Gosport in September 1993, this van appears to display evidence of London & South Western Railway origin. It is wooden-framed with an overall length of 15ft 4in, a wheelbase of 9ft 2in, and is fitted with William Panter's cross-lever brakes. The van is now painted up as a hoarding to advertise the Somerset & Dorset Railway Museum at Washford, where it is now based.

### SNSO No 258

Built in 1923 to a Great Eastern Railway design, probably at Stratford Works, the van carried the LNER number 632516, and is of 10-ton capacity. It was eventually sold off for naval use, from where it was obtained by the WSR in 1985.

### RNAD No 304

Originally from Gosport, and arriving on the railway during September 1993, this ventilated van certainly appears to be of London & South Western Railway origin, possibly built around 1898 to Diagram 1401. It has a timber frame, an overall length of 18 feet, and a wheelbase of 11 feet on Maunsell wooden wheels. Further investigation revealed LSWR Panter & Shepherd mixed axleboxes, LSWR plain buffer castings, and power brakes on both sides. It is now in the care of the S&DRT and is kept at Washford, painted in SR livery and bearing the number 51171.

**RNAD No 305**
Again of LSWR origin, the original numbers are unknown, but it is believed to have been built around 1910 to Diagram 1401. Fitted with wooden-centred Maunsell wheels, it was once vacuum-fitted for main-line running, and is of 8-ton capacity. Believed to have been sold to the Navy in 1940, it was purchased by the S&DRT from Gosport in 1984, and is painted in SR brown livery as No 42106.

**RNAD No 335**
Of LNWR origin, indicated by the distinctive cross struts on the body ends and by the buffer castings, this van is timber-framed and 18 feet long, with a 9ft 10in wheelbase. Purchased from Gosport in September 1993, it is now at Washford.

**SNSO No 535**
Built by S. J. Clay of Long Eaton for the Admiralty in about 1910, this van was used internally at Chatham Dockyard until closure, when it was transferred to Gosport. Purchased privately for preservation in March 1984, it was painted grey and lettered 'G&SW' for use in demonstration goods trains, although there is no historical basis for this.

**LMS No ADM396003**
Built by Metro-Cammell in 1938, under Lot 1154 to Diagram 2026, this van originally carried the number M37103. The Isabel Group purchased the van from Bristol in March 1976, and it is now to be seen at Washford.

**LMS No 179162**
Little is known about this steel-bodied van, but research suggests that it is possibly one of a thousand built for the LMS by four different outside contractors. The building date is 1929/30, to Diagram 1828. The batch was experimental, and eventually superseded by wooden-bodied vans. Now owned by the S&DRT, it is normally kept at Washford.

**GWR No W105493**
Built at Swindon in November 1924 to Diagram Z3, this is a 'Gunpowder Van' (GPV), one of 11 under Lot 935. The original design was based on the 'Iron Minks' and code-named 'CONE'. The wagon bodies were wood with lead lining, all nails used were either brass or copper, and at no point was metal allowed to come into contact with metal to avoid sparks. Withdrawn from Swindon in 1976, it is now owned by the 813 Fund, and is now fully repainted to appear in demonstration goods trains.

**GWR No 2823**
Built by the GWR in 1937 under Lot 1606 to Diagram Y9 and classified

GWR Gunpowder Van No W105493. *Keith Smith*

'Fruit C', these were the last vehicles to use the short-arm brake. Formerly gas-lit, and marked 'Return to Evesham', No 2823 was converted in 1963 to departmental use for rail-warming equipment, and was condemned at Taunton in 1972. Purchased in 1975 for departmental use, it was restored in brown and labelled 'WSR'. Now resplendent in GWR brown, it is used regularly in demonstration freight trains.

**GWR No 16307**

Another example of an early GWR van, this was built in about 1907 to Diagram V12, and is a 'Mink A'. The body length is a standard 16 feet with a 9-foot wheelbase, and the height is 11ft 9in, being the standard dimensions from this diagram onwards.

**GWR No 126779**

Built some time in the second half of the 1930s to Diagram V23, this is a standard 12-ton van with external dimensions as per No 16307. It was purchased from the Royal Ordnance Factory at Puriton, near Bridgwater.

**GWR No 139760**

All the details for this van are as for No 126779 above.

**GWR No 11451**

Originally built by the GWR at Swindon in June 1901 under Lot 418 to Diagram V5, this is a wooden-bodied version of the famous 'Iron Mink'. Only a small number were built to this diagram as they were regarded as having too small a capacity, and subsequent diagrams made provision for a higher roof. Worthy of note is the short-arm brake handle, usually only found on open wagons, but with the push rod outside the wheel, rather than inside. The van was condemned in the early 1960s, and received an internal static number of 064547. Together with four other vans, it was sent to Chipping Norton on the Banbury-Kingham branch until it closed to freight traffic in December 1962, when the stock was dispersed. Purchased for preservation in 1980 by the S&DRT, it can now be seen at Washford.

*Left:* GWR box van No 16307 built c1907.

Below: GWR Box van No 126779. *Keith Smith*

**SR No S48949**
From 1935 until nationalisation in 1948, and afterwards by BR, large numbers of 12-ton box vans were constructed to a standard Southern Railway diagram. This design was little changed over the period, and ours is a typical example. Now in the care of the S&DRT, it can be seen at Washford.

**SR No 1360**
Built under Lot 1031 at Ashford in 1939, this wooden-bodied vehicle was classified as a 'Parcels & Miscellaneous Van' (PMV). Its maximum permitted speed was 70mph, with a total length of 32 feet and a 21-foot wheelbase.

**SR No 1458**
Another PMV, this example was built at Wolverton in 1951 and is used as a store by the Association's Locomotive Department at Williton.

**SR No 1464**
Another PMV built at Wolverton in 1951.

**SR No 1633**
This PMV was built at Ashford/Lancing in 1950.

**SR No 1964**
This PMV was built at Ashford in 1938 under Lot 973, and is used by the Association's Restorations Department at Williton as a paint shop.

**BR(W) No 3450**
Built by BR at Swindon in 1955 under Lot 1771 to an old GWR Diagram Y14, it was classified as a 'Fruit D'. Originally painted red, it ended its BR days in BR blue, but now carries a maroon livery. It was condemned in 1976 at Reading, where it was labelled to work only between Reading NCL yard and Reading station. The van is now privately owned, and can normally be seen at Washford.

**BR No B752355**
This is a standard 12-ton box van built by BR to a Southern Railway diagram. It was purchased by the 1163 Fund in 1973 from Bath, where it was used as a security store on an isolated piece of track running into the GWR goods shed. Transported to Bishops Lydeard and placed behind the signal box, it had the honour of being the first vehicle to arrive on the WSR after closure of the line by BR in January 1971. It is now owned by the 5542 Group.

BR(W) 'Fruit D' No 3450 seen here at Washford. *Keith Smith*

**BR No W94502**
Built in 1960 at Earlestown under Lot 30563 to Diagram 816, this vehicle was classified as a 'Covered Carriage Truck' (CCT) but was later classified as 'NPV'. Appearing in the BR coaching stock list, it weighed 17t 6cwt, had a body length

of 37 feet, a twin-axle wheelbase of 23ft 6in, and a load capacity of 10 tons. Originally privately purchased, the van housed a model railway exhibition at Minehead, which was open to the public, but it is now a store van for the Friends of Minehead Station (FoMS).

### BR No M94917

Again built at Earlestown, but in 1961 under Lot 30651, the technical details of this van are as for No W94502 above. It was obtained from Exeter Carriage & Wagon Works, arriving in July 1981, and after a period of use as general storage and tool transport it was converted into a generator van, and given the code name 'EGOR' – Electricity Generated on Request! For the 2000 Spring Steam Gala the van was painted in maroon livery, and ran in passenger train formations.

### BR No KDB787158

Arriving on the line in October 2002, from Bristol, this is a 20-ton continental ferry van built in Ashford to Diagram 1/227, under Lot No 3472. Both vacuum and Westinghouse brakes are fitted, and it is 41ft 11in long with a wheelbase of 26ft 3in. Owned by the Diesel & Electric Preservation Group, it is based at Williton.

### BR No B784676

Built 1962 at Derby under Lot No 3392 to Diagram 1/217, this was classified as a 12T Ventilated Goods Van. Also owned by the D&EPG, it is a regular sight in the railway's heritage goods train.

BR No KDB787158. *Keith Smith*

Derby-built BR No B784676. *Keith Smith*

## Open wagons

### GWR No 80669

Built by the GWR in 1936 as a ballast open wagon of 10-ton capacity to Diagram P15, it was mostly used for permanent way duties. Latterly the wagon carried an internal use number of 060963, and is now owned by the 813 Fund, forming part of the WSR's heritage goods train.

### GER No 5043

Built in about 1920 by the Great Eastern Railway, and later renumbered 605043 by the LNER, this 10-ton wagon was probably purchased in 1941 by the War Department for use at Bicester when the depot there opened. Purchased privately from the Royal Ordnance Factory at Puriton, near Bridgwater, for preservation, it carried the MoD number 46017.

**LNER No 632516**
Built at Stratford in 1923 to a Great Eastern Railway design, this wagon was sold for Admiralty use at Chatham and Gosport, and was allocated the number SNSO576. It is now privately preserved.

**GWR No 137696**
Acquired from the Naval Dockyard at Rosyth by the 813 Fund, this wagon was built in 1938 under Lot 1314 to Diagram E4. Capable of carrying a 12-ton load, it was an aeroplane propeller wagon, with the telegraphic code 'AERO', constructed as a simple underframe with overall decking incorporating a small opening through which one of the three propeller blades could pass. Triangular cradles were fitted to enable two propellers to be carried side by side. It was converted into an ordinary open wagon later in its life, possibly in the early 1950s.

**MoD No 46242**
Built at Ashford in about 1955, this was part of an MoD order for 50 wagons intended for main-line use. They had through vacuum-pipes, but not fitted with vacuum brakes. Eventually this wagon was sent to the Royal Ordnance Factory at Puriton for internal use, but was found not to be suitable for carrying waste hot ashes from the boiler house. Now privately owned on the WSR, it was initially painted in Southern Railway livery, but for the 2004 Spring Steam Gala it was given a repaint into full MoD livery.

**MoD No 46253**
All the details for this wagon are as for No 46242 above.

**SNSO No 44**
Formerly from the Gosport Admiralty Railway and Chatham Dockyard, this wagon was built by an outside contractor for Admiralty use. Fitted with grease axleboxes, it is now privately owned on the WSR.

**RNAD No 108**
This is a very interesting wagon, which seems to date back to the late 1800s. Now existing as a flat wagon 15ft 1in long, with an 8ft 11in wheelbase, it has four LSWR Panter cast-iron axleboxes and wheelsets of a very old design consisting of wrought iron open spokes cast onto hubs bearing the words 'PATENT SHAFT & AXLETREE Co 1877'. Panter cross-lever brakes on double V-hangers, LSWR plain round

No 46253, one of an MoD order for 50 such wagons. *Keith Smith*

buffer castings and drawbar hooks stamped 'LSWR Co' are all evident. It was built as some form of open wagon, with evidence of uprights and fittings on the frame, but it is not known when or where conversion took place. Now at Washford, it arrived there in September 1993 from Gosport Dockyard.

**RNAD No 119**
Investigation reveals this wagon to be of London, Brighton & South Coast Railway origin, the buffers and mountings, drawbar hook plate, and curved W-irons substantiating that claim. It is a timber-framed four-plank open wagon with a 9ft 2in wheelbase, and is now at Washford, arriving there from Gosport in September 1993. It now carries SR livery as No 24281. The length over headstocks is 15ft 5in, with a 9ft 2in wheelbase.

**RNAD No 184**
A four-plank timber-framed open wagon, this example is of unknown origin. It has self-contained buffers, early open-spoke wheels and a distinctive rectangular wagon label pocket. Purchased from Gosport and arriving at Washford in September 1993, it now carries the livery of NE No 424023. It has a capacity of 10 tons, a length over headstocks of 15ft 10in, and a 9ft 4in wheelbase.

**RNAD No 194**
A four-plank timber-framed open wagon of LNER or even GNR origin, it has a 10-foot wheelbase and early-pattern open-spoke wheelsets. Again purchased from Gosport, it arrived at Washford in September 1993, and now carries the livery of NE No 145741.

## Former Port of Bristol Authority open wagons

Although none of the former Port of Bristol Authority wagons arrived on the WSR with any plates attached, it has been possible to deduce some history by careful examination. Of note is the PoBA numbering scheme. The first two characters indicate the year of purchase, and the last two the next free number in the fleet; the middle character was usually left as '0'. For example, No 61045 was purchased in 1961, and became the PoBA's 45th wagon at the time.

**No 59378**
This is an ex-South Eastern & Chatham Railway eight-plank open wagon dating from around 1920. It has central drop doors with hinges above, where originally side-hinged gates were fitted, and an unusual design of axlebox.

**No 61045**
This ex-LMS five-plank wagon built in 1932 is the only ex-PoBA wagon with full-height central drop doors; the remaining wagons have had their doors cut down by the previous owner for ease of loading.

**No 63015**
A six-plank wagon.

**No 63058**
Also a six-plank wagon.

**No 61078**
Another six-plank open wagon, previous POBA history not known. It is now owned by the D&EPG and on display at Minehead in the livery of Foster Yeoman No 46.

## Tank wagons

**No 401**
The London, Tilbury & Southend Railway first registered this wagon in 1902, as No 231. It has a 10-foot wheelbase, wooden headstocks, and was built to carry 20 tons. The owners, Shell-Mex & BP Ltd, presented the wagon to the S&DRT while the Group was still based at Radstock, and it is now in its care at Washford.

Kindly donated to the railway by the company whose name it carries is tank wagon No 1326. *Keith Smith*

**No 1326**
Originally built in 1918 for the Caledonian Railway, this vehicle was rebuilt in 1942 by the LMS, which renumbered it 26226. It was eventually sold to Esso and given the number 1326. After being restored by Esso into the company's silver livery, the wagon was generously donated to the WSR. With a tare weight of 10t 6cwt, it has a load capacity of 14 tons on a standard 10-foot wheelbase. No 1326 has seen use in the railway's heritage freight train.

**No 1822**
Registered by the LMS in 1939 and given the number 165363, this wagon was later sold to Esso, which renumbered it 1822. The wagon was again kindly donated to the railway after restoration by Esso, and is usually seen at Minehead, but used occasionally on weed-killing trains.

**GWR No 102**
Built at Swindon in 1946 under Lot No 1555, Diagram DD6, it was a glass-lined drinking water tank wagon. It has a 3,000-gallon capacity on a six-wheeled frame.

**GWR No W3018**
Built at Swindon in 1946, this was a glass-lined milk tank wagon to Diagram O57.

Built to carry milk, this is GWR No W3018. *Keith Smith*

# Brake vans

*Above:* Wartime brake van No 49017 is seen at rest in Minehead sidings. *Keith Smith*

*Above right:* LSWR No 12424. *Keith Smith*

## MoD No 49017

Built by the Southern Railway in 1942 for a War Office order, this is a standard SR design with the addition of vacuum brakes, the cylinders being positioned above the frames rather than below, which is the norm for this type of vehicle. No 49017 was registered by the War Office with the SR as No 1024 for main-line operation. Although purchased from 322 Engineer Park, Hessay, Yorkshire, in 1982, it resided at Tidworth prior to 1950, then on the Shropshire & Montgomeryshire Railway until its closure. It was kept in very good condition by the MoD, but some rot was found in the woodwork. Now repainted in grey with white handles and lamp brackets, and black underframes, the body has been repaired and the vacuum brake restored; the latter had been removed by the previous owners as none of its locomotives were so equipped.

## LSWR No 12424

Initially designed by the LSWR as its standard goods brake van, nearly 450 were taken over by the Southern Railway during the post-1923 'Big Four' period. It was a single-balcony brake van with a guard's compartment; part of the body acted as a general goods van, enabling small items of merchandise to be collected and delivered en route, particularly useful on rural branch lines where it allowed one vehicle to perform more than one function. Our example is No 12424, built at Eastleigh in 1900; the SR renumbering it 54885 and issued Diagram 1541 to the class. It was reported to have been working in the Herne Hill area before being sold to the Longmoor Military Railway and renumbered AD82020. When the LMR closed, the van was moved to Liss (May 1970), Eastleigh (October 1971), then to the East Somerset Railway in November 1973. In 1988 it was purchased for display at the S&DRT site at Washford, where it now resides in a restored condition. Its rated capacity is 10 tons, the total length is 21 feet and the width 7ft 9½in, with a wheelbase of 10ft 6in. The frames and body are of wooden construction.

**GWR No 68765**
Built by the GWR in 1942 to Diagram AA20, this van was purchased from South Wales by the 813 Fund and arrived on the WSR in 1989. All GWR brake vans were given the telegraphic code name 'TOAD'. The van has been completely restored in GWR dark grey livery, and is used regularly on both demonstration freight trains and engineering trains.

**GWR No 56631**
Built by the GWR in 1918 to Diagram AA13 under Lot 840, it was later converted to a sleeping and messing van for engineers' use. Privately purchased from Radyr, near Cardiff, in late 1989, it arrived on the WSR in February 1990. Originally placed on a small length of track at Stogumber, it is now in store awaiting a decision on its future.

**W114751**
Built in 1934 at Swindon to Diagram AA20 under Lot 1171, this is a standard 20T, 16-foot-wheelbase, single-veranda GWR 'TOAD' goods brake van. It was converted to run as a tool van for a crane at Leyton, East London, but was later bought for preservation by the owner of Rowden Mill Station – see W80976 above – where it was restored to original condition. Put on the market again in mid-2015, the new owner is a WSR supporter, and the brake van was moved to the WSR on 21 September 2015 to join the existing GWR 'TOAD' No 68765 in the heritage freight train.

**LMS No M732525**
Built in 1949 by BR at Derby to a standard LMS design (Diagram 2068) under Lot 1518, it is 24 feet long over the headstocks, and has a 16-foot wheelbase and a 20-ton tare weight. It arrived on the WSR during 1998 after a life of approximately 20 years at the ROF, Puriton, near Bridgwater.

**BR No B952527**
Built under Lot 2606 to Diagram 1/506 at Faverdale in 1954, this is a standard 20-ton goods brake van developed from an ex-LNER design. Its total length is 27 feet over the buffers with a 16-foot body and wheelbase. Fitted with open verandas at each end of the 10-foot cabin, a screw brake and stove are fitted inside. It arrived on the WSR in February 2004 from the Dart Valley Light Railway.

**BR No B953089**
Built under Lot 2741 to Diagram 1/504 at Faverdale in 1955, this is another standard 20-ton goods brake van from the ex-LNER design – all other details are as No B952527 above. The van has been repaired and is now painted in BR bauxite livery, being used regularly as part of the railway's heritage freight train.

## Bogie wagons

**GWR No 32742**
Built to Diagram J21, under Lot 1273, this is a 'Bogie Bolster' wagon with the telegraphic code name 'MACAW B'. Rated to carry a 30-ton load, it is used primarily on engineering trains.

**GWR No 32822**
The details for this wagon are as for No 32742 above.

**GWR No 84685**
Again built to Diagram J21, but under Lot 831, this wagon was purchased from Rosyth Dockyard by the 813 Fund.

**MoD No 84003**
Built by the Midland Railway for the War Department to Diagram D1095 under Lot 931, the purpose of these bogie wagons was the transportation of First World War tanks. They had the normal diamond-pattern frame bogies of the period, but a very unusual feature of the design was the screw jacks fitted to assist with the drive-on loading of tanks. Four jacks were fitted to make contact with the rail, two in the middle section and one at each end, hung from the buffer beam on a U-shaped bracket. During loading and unloading the jacks were screwed down to take the weight off the springs and prevent them sagging. Code-named 'RECTANK', various railway companies built many of these wagons for the War Department in 1918, and they were shipped to the continent, although the war had ended before they were used to any great extent. Many were sold off to railway companies, while others went to military stores depots in Great Britain, where they were used internally as well as on the main-line network. The Longmoor Military Railway also had some on its own stock list for training purposes.

At the onset of the Second World War a number were sent to France with the British Expeditionary Force, but were lost in the hostilities. When the war was over, those left intact were returned and re-entered service, but as no records were kept we have no knowledge if our examples made the journey. Purchased from Long Marston in July 1981, this wagon was initially preserved on the Gloucestershire Warwickshire Railway, but was moved to the WSR in November 1986, where it is used mainly for permanent way duties.

**MoD No 84006**
All details are as for No 84003 above.

**MoD No 8080**
Built in 1942 for the War Department by Metropolitan-Cammell Ltd at Saltley, this wagon was designated as a 'WARFLAT'. Few records were kept by the military as to the use and location of this vehicle, but it saw service at Bicester before being transferred to Marchwood, Southampton. Jacks are fitted to facilitate easier loading as described for the 'Rectanks' above, and it is of 50-ton capacity. Purchased by the Home Counties Group of the West Somerset Railway Association, it arrived on the line in late 1998, and is intended to be restored for use in demonstration freight trains.

**LUL No 447**
Purchased from London Transport in 1997, this wagon is 70 feet long and is built to 'tube' dimensions. Underground stock coupling gear is fitted, together with buffers that can be hinged back out of the way; these have now been removed from one end. It is used on permanent way and engineering trains, where the low deck height proves very useful.

**LUL No 483**
Details for this vehicle are the same as for No 447 above. The two wagons are permanently coupled together at the ends from which the buffers have been removed.

**BR No DB978032**
Purchased from EWS at Fairwater Yard, Taunton, in October 2002, this is a 34-ton bogie wagon designated 'TURBOT'. Built at Shildon 1982/83 to Lot No 4021, it last saw service during 1997-98 on the Westbury to Minehead stone trains run as part of the Minehead Sea Defence scheme. Moved to Bishops Lydeard by road, it is now used regularly on permanent way trains.

**BR No DB978037**
Details are as for No DB978032 above.

**BR No DB978105**
Details are as for No DB978032 above.

**BR No DB978348**
Details are as for No DB978032 above.

**BR No DB978622**
Details are as for No DB978032 above.

## Ballast hoppers

**BR No 983652**
Built by Metropolitan-Cammell Ltd in 1960 to Diagram 1/586 under Lot 3331 and given the telegraphic code name 'CATFISH', it has a tare weight of 19 tons. It was purchased by WSR plc in 1995, and is used by the Permanent Way Department.

Ballast hopper No 983652. *Keith Smith*

**BR No 993529**
The details for this are as for No 983652 above, except that it was built in 1959 under Lot 2929.

**BR No 983909**
Built at Shildon in 1961 to Diagram 1/581 under Lot No 3340, this wagon was classified as a 'DOGFISH' and was purchased by the West Somerset Railway during the summer of 2003. Delivered in mid-September in the former 'Transrail' Sector grey livery, a repaint in the D&EPG Williton workshops to a bauxite red body with black underframes enabled the wagon to run in the heritage goods train for the first time at the 2003 Autumn Steam Gala.

**BR No 983290**
Built by Charles Roberts in 1959 to Diagram 1/587 under Lot No 2824, this wagon is also a 'DOGFISH', and is now owned by the West Somerset Railway.

**BR No 993592**
Details are as for No 983290 above, except that this was built at Shildon in 1960, under Lot No 3255.

# Other wagons

Sleeper Wagon No DW100678. *Keith Smith*

## BR 'Lowmac' No B904146

This is a 21-ton low machine wagon ('Lowmac') built at Shildon during 1960 to Diagram No 2/240, under Lot No 3254. It arrived at Williton during October 2002 from Bristol, where it had seen service with First Great Western as a transporter wagon for HST engines. It is now under the care of the Diesel & Electric Preservation Group.

## GWR Sleeper Wagon No DW100678

Built at Swindon in April 1939 to Diagram T12 under Lot No 1313, it was intended for use by the Permanent Way Department for transporting sleepers The wagon later acquired sides, and was allocated to Taunton Concrete Works, from where it was obtained by the WSR.

## B900118

Built in 1959 at Shildon to Diagram 2/530 under Lot 3252, this wagon is classified as a 'FLATROL'. Its length over buffers is 37ft 10in, and it has a 24-foot wheelbase and a 21-ton capacity. It is privately owned, and is used on works trains.

'Flatrol' No B900118. *Keith Smith*

# Cranes

## GWR Hand Crane No 264

A vehicle with a very obscure history, it was built at Swindon at an unknown date. It was purchased by the 813 Fund from Severn Tunnel Junction, and moved to the WSR in the autumn of 1982. The crane has a lifting capacity of 5 tons, and is used for general engineering work on any part of the railway. Coupled to the crane is a match truck, No 541, again of unknown origin, but once a four-plank open wagon.

## No ADRW96500

This vehicle consists of a bogie well wagon built in 1942 by the Gloucester Carriage & Wagon Company, and registered by the LMS. A plate shows the owner as being 'M.S.' (perhaps Ministry of Supply?). A 45-foot 'Atlas' hydraulic crane has subsequently been fitted, powered by an onboard diesel engine, although the vehicle is not self-propelled. It is regularly used on engineering duties throughout the railway.

## Coles Crane PW Dept No 1

One of the major items of rolling stock used by the WSR's Permanent Way Department is this Coles diesel-electric self-propelled crane. With a lifting capacity of 3 tons, it was purchased from the Port of Bristol Authority during the summer of 1987. It is used throughout the line, and even manages to star in the WSR's 'Days Out With Thomas' weekends on occasions.

When heavy lifting up to 3 tons is required the Permanent Way department call on No 1, seen here at Minehead. *Keith Smith*

# Miscellaneous stock

## Preserved bodies

### Somerset & Dorset Joint Railway 3rd Class Coach No 98

Built by Cravens of Sheffield in 1984, it was transferred to Southern Railway ownership in 1930, renumbered in its stock list as No 1419, and probably allocated to Set No 705. Remarkably, the body was still carrying the Prussian Blue livery when withdrawn from service in August 1939, and was sold to a private owner. Together with No 114 (see below) it was converted into part of a bungalow at Aldingbourne, near Chichester. The S&DRT was already aware of the existence of the bodies and, when the site owner had a property built on the same plot, the Trust was given permission to recover and move them to Washford. Due to the protection provided by a roof and side sheeting, the body of No 98 had the best preserved example of 1920s S&DJR livery, but internally much had been altered and removed. A six-wheeled underframe from an ex-LMS fish van now supports the body.

### Somerset & Dorset Joint Railway 3rd Class Coach No 114

Built at Highbridge in 1890, this coach had a very similar history to that of No 98 above, except that it became No 1423 in the Southern Railway stock list.

### Somerset & Dorset Joint Railway Brake Van No 9

Believed to be a shorter version of the Somerset & Dorset Railway 'Mail brake' design, this body had been living in a field at Highbridge for about 70 years. Having a body length of some 16 feet and a height of 6 feet, the wheelbase is assumed to have been 9 feet, with a tare weight of 10 tons. Its building date is not known, but could be the mid-1870s. It was withdrawn in 1929, when it was moved to its field location. Preservation commenced over the weekend of 25-26 February 2001, when S&DRT members arrived to dismantle and move the body to a private site for storage. Due to its age and condition, only parts of the salvaged vehicle are suitable for re-use – the remainder will be used to produce templates for new parts. The chassis of No 535 has been donated to the project.

# Spotter's corner

Harking back to the days when steam formed most of the motive power on Britain's national network, and the loco-spotters books made famous by Ian Allan were the 'must have' item for railway enthusiasts, we provide here a listing of numbers contained within these pages. Why not revisit those days with a pen and ruler to underline those spotted on visits to the railway?

## Former main-line steam locomotives

4110
4160
4561
4936 *Kinlet Hall*
6960 *Raveningham Hall*
7821 *Ditcheat Manor*
7828 *Odney Manor*
9351
44422
53808

## Former Industrial steam locomotives

1788 *Kilmersdon*
1219

## Former main-line diesel locomotives

D1010 *Western Campaigner*
D1661 *North Star*
D2133
D2271
D4107
D6566
D6575
D7017
D7018
D9518
D9526

## Former industrial diesel locomotives

24
1
2

## Diesel multiple units

DMU 115
DMU 117

## Rolling stock

### Mark I First Open (FO)

3018
3058
3131

### Mark I Second Open (SO)

4814

### Mark I Tourist Second Open (TSO)

| | |
|---|---|
| 4260 | 4884 |
| 4346 | 4909 |
| 4419 | 4911 |
| 4435 | 4956 |
| 4449 | 4987 |
| 4599 | 5002 |
| 4660 | 5024 |
| 4875 | 5025 |
| 4876 | 5030 |

### Mark I Corridor Second (SK)

| | |
|---|---|
| 24985 | 25323 |
| 25308 | 25454 |

### Mark I Brake Corridor Second (BSK)

35257
35408

### Mark I Brake Second Open (BSO)

| | |
|---|---|
| 9227 | 9380 |
| 9278 | |

### Mark I Corridor Brake First (BFK)

W17015

### Mark I Brake Corridor Composite (BCK)

21174

### Mark I Miniature Buffet

1804

### Undefined Restaurant Car (RUB)

1909

**District Engineer' Saloon**
W80976

**Mark 1 Gangwayed Brake (BG)**
80736 80742 80972

**Ex-BR No M31407M**
XDB 977037

**High Security Brake Van**
94442

## Former GWR Passenger Stock

**Corridor Third**
2573 3639 3885
2578 3668 3980

**Brake Corridor Composite**
6705

**Corridor Composite**
7740

**Bogie Gangwayed Milk Van ('Siphon G')**
W2980 W1046

**Auto-trailer**
W169

**Sleeping car**
9038

## Former Somerset & Dorset Joint Railway passenger stock

**1st Class Passenger Coach**
4

## Freight Stock

**Box vans**

| | |
|---|---|
| 47983 | 11451 |
| 229 | S48949 |
| 258 | 1360 |
| 304 | 1458 |
| 305 | 1464 |
| 335 | 1633 |
| 535 | 1964 |
| 396003 | 3450 |
| 179162 | B752355 |
| W105493 | W94502 |
| 2823 | M94917 |
| 16307 | KDB787158 |
| 126779 | B784676 |
| 139760 | |

**Open wagons**

| | |
|---|---|
| 80669 | 44 |
| 5043 | 108 |
| 632516 | 119 |
| 137696 | 184 |
| 46242 | 194 |
| 46253 | |

**Former PoBA open wagons**

| | |
|---|---|
| 59378 | 63015 |
| 61045 | 63058 |
| 61078 | |

**Tank wagons**

| | |
|---|---|
| 401 | 102 |
| 1326 | W3018 |
| 1822 | |

**Brake vans**

| | |
|---|---|
| 49017 | W114751 |
| 12424 | M732525 |
| 68765 | B952527 |
| 56631 | B953089 |

**Bogie wagons**

| | |
|---|---|
| 32742 | 483 |
| 32822 | DB978032 |
| 84685 | DB978037 |
| 84003 | DB978105 |
| 84006 | DB978348 |
| 8080 | DB978622 |
| 447 | |

**Ballast hoppers**

| | |
|---|---|
| 983652 | 983290 |
| 993529 | 993592 |
| 983909 | |

**Other wagons**
B904146
B900118
DW100678

**Cranes**
GWR Hand Crane No 264
Coles Crane PW Dept No 1
ADRW96500

**Preserved bodies**
Somerset & Dorset Joint Railway 3rd Class Coach No 98

Somerset & Dorset Joint Railway 3rd Class Coach No 114

Somerset & Dorset Joint Railway Brake Van No 9